5th & 6th Grade Smart Pages

Wes Haystead and Tom Prinz

Gospel Light

EDITORIAL STAFF

Publisher, William T. Greig • **Senior Consulting Publisher,** Dr. Elmer L. Towns
Publisher, Research, Planning and Development, Billie Baptiste
Senior Editor, Lynnette Pennings, M.A.
Senior Consulting Editors, Dr. Gary S. Greig, Wesley Haystead, M.S.Ed.
Editor, Theological and Biblical Issues, Bayard Taylor, M.Div.
Writers, Sheryl Haystead, Wesley Haystead, Tom Prinz
Associate Technical Editor, Linda Mattia • **Assistant Editor,** Noni Pendleton
Designer, Carolyn Thomas • **Illustrators,** Curtis Dawson, Chizuko Yasuda

Gospel Light

CONTENTS

HOW TO USE THIS BOOK
DEAR TEACHER,
THINK OF THIS BOOK AS YOUR—

LIBRARY OF RESOURCES

Cataloged by subject, always at your fingertips, providing you with vital, concise information about teaching juniors effectively.

YELLOW PAGES

Just as you grab your phone book when you need a product or service, grab this manual when you need concise, down-to-earth information which can help you or your staff do a better job.

TOOL KIT

Stocked with useful, practical training helps which fit the needs of busy teachers—and leaders—of the preteens God has entrusted to your care.

RECIPE FILE

Filled with ideas you can use for a wide variety of occasions when your staff needs nurture for their vital ministry with fifth- and sixth-grade students.

TRAINING TEACHERS AND LEADERS: A ONE-YEAR PLAN

1. **From the Contents pages, select the topics of most value to your Junior staff.**

2. **Schedule monthly (or at least bimonthly or quarterly) meetings with your staff, selecting one of the topics for each meeting.**

Choose one of these ideas for each meeting:
- Use the article(s) to prepare a presentation about the topic. Distribute copies for teachers to take home.
- Distribute copies of an article in advance of the meeting so teachers will be prepared to discuss ways to implement suggestions.
- Distribute copies of an article as teachers arrive. Teachers form small groups and discuss the article.

Here are some questions you can use to encourage discussion:
- What are some things the article mentions that you are already doing?
- How might your next class be different if you put into practice one idea from this article?
- What three ideas from this article are most helpful for your class?
- What difficulty might you face in implementing an idea from this article? Who can you talk to about ways to overcome this difficulty?

3. **Select articles from this manual to use in a periodic newsletter to communicate with your Junior staff.**
- Feature the topic for the next staff meeting.
- Include one or more other articles which will benefit your teachers.
- Identify major announcements and events to include in each issue.
- Identify several human-interest features to catch attention (i.e., "Teacher of the Month," "Class in the Spotlight," "Ideas Worth Sharing," "Available Teaching Resources" [listing books, videos, filmstrips, supplies, etc. which correlate with the coming month's lessons], "Welcome to the Team" [introducing new staff members], etc.).

A SAMPLE ONE-YEAR TRAINING/COMMUNICATING PLAN FOR JUNIOR TEACHERS/LEADERS

MONTH	TOPIC	PAGE
September	Age-Level Characteristics of Fifth and Sixth Graders	**11**
October	How Juniors Learn Best	**24**
November	Building Relationships with Juniors	**39**
December	Behavior Challenges Throughout the Session	**14**
January	Leading a Good Discussion	**17**
February	Learning Activities—What Are They?	**27**
March	Connecting the Bible to Real Life	**9**
April	Bible Memory with Juniors	**8**
May	Leading Your Preteen Students to Christ	**44**
June	Teaching Juniors to Pray	**37**
July	Learning Activities—Games	**31**
August	Motivate Your Students to Learn	**36**

OTHER STUFF TO DO WITH THIS BOOK

1. **Provide helpful information for parents as well as teachers.**
- See "Positive Parenting for the Preteen Years" (pages 97-144) for articles to help support and educate parents with children entering these crucial years.
- Use the articles in a regular newsletter to parents or as the basis of a parenting support group or class.
- Use the clip art (pages 147-157) to enhance the impact of your printed flier or newsletter.

2. **Improve educational facilities.**
Look under "Facilities" in the contents.

3. **Choose curriculum best suited for preteens.**
Look under "Curriculum" in the contents.

4. **Help teachers:**
- make better use of curriculum resources
- stimulate interest in Bible memory
- nurture preteens in meaningful prayer and personal Bible study
- encourage missions awareness

5. **Provide selected articles to include in a packet for prospective and new teachers.**
A few brief, thoughtfully compiled articles can make a new teacher's first sessions productive and enjoyable. For example:
  The Teacher's Role
  Teacher's Personal Bible Study
  Age-Level Characteristics of Fifth & Sixth Graders
  A Non-Typical Session
  The Teaching-Learning Process

Obviously, these aren't the only articles which are appropriate for a new teacher. However, it is better to give a new person a few items which he or she will read and remember than many items which will overwhelm the person and end up being ignored.

6. **Let your own creativity stimulate you to think of other ways to use the resources in this manual.**
For example, tape record an article and distribute the cassette among your staff and/or have it available to give to new teachers.

TROUBLESHOOTING GUIDE FOR TEACHERS

BY WESLEY HAYSTEAD, M.S.ED.

This section contains dozens of concise, informative articles dealing with common problems faced by teachers of fifth and sixth graders.

Use this information in both preventive and prescriptive form: for teacher training **before** problems occur, and as a remedy to problem situations **already** in place.

Just photocopy the articles of your choice and distribute; or use selected topics as the basis for teacher training sessions. Either way, it's a snap!

ABOUT THE AUTHOR:

Wes Haystead is vice president of Lowell Brown Enterprises and has a master's degree in educational psychology from the University of Southern California. He is former curriculum editor for *Focus on the Family*, former senior editor for Gospel Light and has been minister of education at two churches. Haystead is the creator of many teaching resources and the author of several books, including *5 Habits of Happy Families* and *Teaching Your Child About God*. Wes lives in Southern California with his wife, Sheryl, and their children.

BIBLE MEMORY WITH JUNIORS

Some teachers approach Bible memory work as though Psalm 119:11 says, "Thy Word have I hid in my heart that I might get a star on my chart."

They seem to confuse Bible verses with vitamin pills or insurance: "You may not understand this verse now, but later on you'll appreciate it."

Then there are those who seem committed to transmitting traditions: "I had to learn Bible verses when I was a kid. Now it's your turn."

And then there are the ones who hold an open Bible, following along as the students recite. Their explanation: "Kids are good at memorizing; adults aren't!"

Or the teachers who put up large charts on which a few students have earned a vast array of stars, while the rest of the class obviously gave up after the second week.

Last are teachers who prompt juniors through recitations of verses without giving any attention to the meaning or application. In far too many cases, Bible memorization is treated as though it were such an unpleasant thing to do that students will only attempt it if given a prize for the effort.

Discovering truths from God's Word can be an exciting and rewarding experience for fifth and sixth graders. Some students may memorize easily. Others may have difficulty recalling all the words, but can still clearly understand the meaning of the passage. Be sensitive to the learning level and learning style of each student. Each is an individual and has a different capacity to memorize and recall.

Here are some ideas for helping juniors understand and memorize God's Word.

◆ Refer to phrases and concepts from Bible verses and passages as often as possible in your natural conversation and discussion during each session.

◆ Ask questions to check a student's understanding of a specific Bible passage. For example, "How would you say this verse in your own words? How might you explain this verse to a younger child? How would you explain it to a friend who was not familiar with the Bible? What are ways these verses can help you at school? in the neighborhood? with your family? What do you think is the most important word in this verse? Why?"

◆ Divide a passage into meaningful segments, focusing on one phrase or sentence at a time. To prompt meaningful recollection of a phrase or sentence, ask questions such as, "What does the passage say about...?" "What will happen if...?"

◆ To aid in memorizing a longer passage, suggest that students memorize the last phrase or sentence first, then add each preceding one until the passage has been learned. This approach works well because people tend to have the most difficulty remembering the end of a passage. By learning the end first, that part of the passage will be repeated most often, and students will remember it easily.

◆ Occasionally share situations in which knowing God's Word has helped you. Repeat a specific Bible verse that has special significance for you.

◆ Use the variety of ways Bible passages are presented and discussed in your curriculum. Games, learning activities and songs encourage understanding and practical application of each Bible passage. As you lead juniors in activities, encourage them to memorize God's Word, and give honest encouragement for each student's efforts.

◆ Rather than individual memorization contests which often discourage juniors for whom memorization is difficult, challenge your students to work together to achieve a class goal. For example, explain that when a passage has been memorized by at least half of the class, you will provide a pizza, popcorn or donut party. Make the first goal one that should be achievable within a month. The second goal can require additional time. Provide a visual reminder of the goal and a means for students to record their progress. For example, students may draw a slice of pizza or donut on a poster to show each point earned.

Above all, remember that your own attitude toward God's Word and your memorization of Bible verses will have the greatest effect on juniors as you encourage them to "hide God's Word in their hearts" (see Psalm 119:11).

CONNECTING THE BIBLE TO REAL LIFE

Can a preteen—in our world of television, video games, and computer access to the world-wide web—be attracted to an ancient book describing vastly different cultures and lifestyles?

Can the interest of a junior be captured by stories he or she has heard or read before?

What good are age-old Bible stories for kids surrounded by drugs, violence, immorality, pollution and secularization?

Because the Bible is a book about God's dealings with real people in a wide variety of settings and situations, it speaks to all people, including preteens, in all cultures and times. The hurdle we face as teachers is how to help students connect Scripture events to the problems of today. Here are three helpful tips in getting over this hurdle:

1. FIND THE COMMON LINK

The more closely a Bible story or verse connects with a personal experience of a student, the more impact the Scriptures will have on the student's understanding, attitude and actions. For example, the story of the Good Samaritan is easy to connect to a kid's life. Most kids have had incidents of being hurt, and then helped by someone's kindness. All have faced the choice of helping someone else in need or going on about their own business. Almost any Bible incident can capture the interest of juniors when linked to their own current interests and problems.

2. FOCUS ON THE STUDENT'S LIFE

Many teachers struggle with getting juniors interested in the Bible because they approach it like a history book. They talk about dead people from another time and a far-distant place, so that learning Bible facts takes on the flavor of preparing for a Bible trivia game.

God repeatedly made it clear that He spoke to people and had His messages written down in order to show people the way to live abundant, godly lives. But what about problems not dealt with in the Bible? How can the Bible help juniors deal with problems like drugs, sexual abuse, affluence, poverty, absent parents, exploitative advertising, violence, pollution, etc.? While a verse or two may touch on these or related topics, few if any Bible stories explicitly address many modern issues.

However, the more a student comes to know God through His Word, the more God equips that child to become the kind of person who can deal positively with life's challenges. To talk to juniors about the evils of drugs without introducing them to the God who can fulfill all their deepest longings is to leave them without the inner strength needed to stand firm against temptation.

3. EMPHASIZE THE REAL APPEAL OF BIBLE LEARNING

Some people think the only way to make the Bible interesting to juniors is to enlist a masterful storyteller, present skits, throw in lots of jokes or retell the story in a modern setting. While unusual approaches can be effective in capturing attention (especially with "jaded juniors" who have "seen it all"), Scripture has very powerful appeals of its own which need only to be emphasized to receive an eager hearing.

◆ **The Bible is true.** In a world where people seek meaning in fiction, fantasy and formulas, the Bible shows human affairs from the unique perspective of the Creator.

◆ **The Bible touches our lives.** God's Spirit speaks to us through this book. Juniors desperately need to learn to begin reading the Bible for themselves, discovering God's personal concern about them as unique individuals.

◆ **The people are real.** People are fascinating. Juniors will go to any lengths to find a friend on a boring afternoon. This interest in people is easily put to work in capturing interest in the Bible, simply by taking the names off the page and helping them come to life in the student's mind.

◆ **The Bible shows God at work.** It shows the God of the universe involving Himself in people's lives, revealing His character and His plans for us. Talk about interesting! No video game can compete with that!

The teacher who sees God's hand in a narrative, who has discovered the personal impact of a Bible passage, who has put God's truth into practice—that teacher will find juniors eager to learn what God's Word has to say.

TEACHER'S PERSONAL BIBLE STUDY

In preparing your lesson, it's easy to spend most of your time planning activities and collecting materials. Busy teachers may find it difficult to focus their thoughts on the meaning and purpose of a passage to be taught, overlooking the rich benefits to be gained from personal Bible study. However, juniors will quickly sense if you are just going through the motions of studying the Bible with them, or if you are enthusiastic about the passage because it has in some way influenced your thoughts and actions. Use this simple outline as a tool in making personal Bible study rewarding for yourself as well as your students.

Bible Passage:

1. What are the key words, phrases and ideas in this passage?

2. What do these key words, phrases and ideas mean? Write several of them in your own words.

3. How does this passage apply to contemporary life?
For people in general:

For me personally:

For students in my class:

AGE-LEVEL CHARACTERISTICS OF FIFTH AND SIXTH GRADERS

PHYSICAL

Fifth and sixth graders have mastered most basic physical skills, are active and curious, and seek a variety of new experiences. Rapid growth can cause some 11-year-olds to tire easily. Gradually—and at times, not so gradually—many juniors are beginning to look more like teenagers than children. Even when the physical changes of puberty have not yet occurred, the patterns of dress, hair styles, speech, and mannerisms are consciously patterned after those of teens.

Teaching Tips: Most 11-year-old boys will still participate in activities with girls, but the marked differences in maturity between younger boys and older girls poses a challenge in getting junior boys and girls to work and play together. This is a good age for exploration and research activities. Use a variety of active, creative ways to explore Bible content and to apply Bible truths to life.

EMOTIONAL

Younger juniors are usually cooperative, easygoing, content, friendly and agreeable. Most adults enjoy working with this age group. Even though both girls and boys begin to think about their future as adults, their interests tend to differ significantly. Be aware of behavioral changes that result from the 11-year-old's emotional struggles in coping with rapid growth

and "raging hormones." Older juniors are beginning to experience unsteady emotions and often shift from one mood to another.

Teaching Tips: Changes of feelings require patient understanding from adults. Give many opportunities to make choices with only a few necessary limits. Take time to listen as juniors share their experiences and problems with you.

SOCIAL

Friendships and activities with peers flourish. Juniors draw together and away from adults in the desire for independence. Conflicts with parents are not uncommon, and even those who still like their parents may feel this somehow makes them odd. The junior wants to be a part of a same-sex group and usually does not want to stand alone in competition.

Teaching Tips: Juniors no longer automatically talk about whatever they are thinking, so keeping communication open is of prime importance. Listen, ask questions and avoid being judgmental. Plan learning activities in which students work cooperatively to complete a task. Encouraging boys and girls to be a part of the same small group, even if for a short segment of the session, helps prevent discipline problems.

INTELLECTUAL

Juniors are highly curious and very verbal! They are able to express ideas and feelings in creative ways. Making ethical decisions becomes a chal-

lenging task as they begin to think beyond the rules to the reasons for them. By 11 years, juniors are beginning to be able to reason abstractly. They begin to think of themselves as adults, and, at the same time, question adult concepts. Hero worship is strong.

Teaching Tips: Include lots of opportunities for talking, questioning and discussing in a safe, accepting environment. These are good years for poetry, songs, drama, stories, drawing and painting. Juniors need encouragement, rather than criticism, when they express ideas and feelings which show they are questioning what they have been told. They enjoy the challenge of exploring the implications of Bible stories they learned "as children."

SPIRITUAL

Fifth and sixth graders can have deep feelings of love for God, and are able to establish and carry out a consistent, but brief, personal quiet time. Juniors can share the good news of Jesus with a friend and are capable of involvement in evangelism and service projects. They may seek guidance from God to make everyday and long-range decisions.

Teaching Tips: Provide opportunities for juniors to make choices and decisions based on Bible concepts. Plan prayer, Bible reading and worship experiences. Involve juniors in work and service projects.

IT'S A KIDS' WORLD AFTER ALL

Teachers of fifth and sixth graders sometimes feel as though they are dealing with creatures from an alien planet.

The world inhabited by children, although sharing much of the good and bad of the world shaped by adults, is often uniquely their own. In order to understand the children we teach, we must seek to understand the world which has shaped them.

CHARACTERISTICS OF A CHILD'S WORLD TODAY

1. A child's world is only a few years old.

All of the momentous events of human experience, including most of the earth-shattering events of our own lifetimes, are ancient history to a sixth grader. Anything that occurred more than two or three years ago are known to the child by hearsay, if at all.

Therefore, the child's most intense interest focuses on the present. And a child's perceptions, beliefs, and understandings are forged through experiences far more than through explanations about the past.

2. A child's world is in, but not of, the world of adults.

Children are surrounded by adults, dependent on adults, intensely curious about adults, yet they are not miniature adults. Children spend a great deal of time pretending to be adults, but they also are keenly aware that they are not adults. Nor are they totally sure they really want to ever become adults.

Thus, children are often unmoved by logic which seems eminently reasonable to adults, often confounding adults by doing things which seem so, so...*childish!*

3. A child's world is marked by energy and imagination.

Adults often idealize this aspect of childhood, fondly recalling some "carefree" times of fantasy and wonder. Perhaps as a refuge from a seeming barrage of adult talking heads, children learn to pursue and cherish their world of private thoughts. Two or three kids together are bound to generate a lot of ideas and activity!

Consequently, children are skilled at "tuning out" what adults say, preferring their own restless inventiveness to what often seems to be adult stodginess.

4. A child's world is marred by life-threatening forces.

On the one hand, many centuries-old scourges no longer threaten our children. Many diseases no longer claim vast numbers of young lives. Child-labor laws protect children from being exploited in factories.

On the other hand, the contemporary scourges of drugs, divorce, gangs, abuse, violence (both in real life and in the media) pose major risks to healthy development. The rapid pace of change, whether positive or negative, adds to the stress of life for both children and adults.

TIPS FOR COMMUNICATING BETWEEN OUR WORLD AND THEIRS

1. It is not necessary to "be up on all the latest" in order to teach juniors.

An adult who has no idea about local gangs or current pop stars can feel very "out of it" around a group of pre-adolescents. Hearing students toss around unfamiliar terms for various drugs can certainly be shocking. While it's good to know as much as possible about the child's world, children do not need every adult in their lives to be walking encyclopedias on contemporary youth culture. What they need most are adults who care.

2. Listen and observe.

Teachers tend to think they should talk a lot. Unfortunately, talking is not a good way to learn from others. Effective teachers do as much careful listening and observing as they do talking. And a good portion of that talking is asking questions designed to provide more opportunities for listening. Young people learn to trust people who care enough to really listen.

3. Focus on relationships.

Advice is cheap, but a friend in need is a friend indeed. These old sayings may be clichés, but they capsulize the core of effective teaching. Most students are not very likely to be lastingly influenced by a teacher's words, but a teacher's friendship is priceless.

4. Look for potential, not perfection.

The many differences between adults and children often contribute to an "us versus them" mentality. As a result, adults "bug" kids, and kids annoy adults. When we are frustrated because children are not more like adults (responsible, thoughtful, etc.), we criticize them for their shortcomings. And that makes the separation even greater. It is far better if adults spend time and energy looking for whatever is positive in the child, not emphasizing what is lacking.

CHOOSING CURRICULUM FOR JUNIORS

Many church leaders have only recently become aware of the great value of small-group experiences for adults and youth. Among those who minister to children, small groups have long been known to be a powerfully effective means of influencing young lives to follow Christ. However, many teachers do not take full advantage of smaller groups, tending to conduct their sessions the same way they would with a large crowd.

In choosing curriculum materials for preteens, look for resources which aid teachers in making the most of small-group learning opportunities. (In teaching juniors, up to eight students per teacher allows for easy implementation of small-group procedures. Each additional student added to a group makes such approaches more difficult.)

1. EMPHASIS ON PARTICIPATION

Juniors learn best when they are actively involved. One of the great values of small groups with preteens is the potential for maximum participation by each student. Therefore, look for teacher and student materials which emphasize a variety of ways to meaningfully involve every student. In addition to intriguing activities which capture interest and motivate participation, quality curriculum for juniors will incorporate in every session very practical tips on guiding students as active learners, not as passive observers.

2. GUIDANCE FOR BUILDING RELATIONSHIPS

Every child needs a sense of belonging, and positive experiences in small groups are vital to building connections with others. Quality curriculum provides ideas to help each student build solid friendships with adult leaders as well as with peers. Look for activities which stress cooperative learning and stimulate awareness of others in the group. Whether students only see each other once a week or are already best of friends, most teachers need help in knowing what to do to promote mutual respect and affection.

3. STIMULATION OF TEACHER/STUDENT INTERACTION

Teachers need feedback from students to determine their needs, interests and levels of understanding. Students need feedback from teachers, both in measuring learning and in recognition of their individuality. Without thoughtful preparation, far too much teacher/student dialog sounds like an examination in which the adult is evaluating and grading the student's responses. Quality curriculum provides teachers with thought-provoking questions and comments which encourage juniors to honestly share their thoughts and feelings. Look for resources which help teachers open up students' awareness of how Scripture applies to all areas of life.

4. RECOGNITION OF ABILITY AND INTEREST DIFFERENCES

No two juniors are identical, even if they are twins. Each one is unique. Even in a very small group, there will always be a range of interests, abilities and understandings among the group members. Quality curriculum is designed to help teachers accommodate diversity. For example, look for points in the session where students are free to select from among two or more alternatives. Thus, the junior who has difficulty reading or writing is not pressured into a task where the likely result is failure. Instead, each student should be able to experience success—even those with no previous church or Sunday School background.

5. EMPHASIS ON SPIRITUAL VITALITY AS KEY TO SUCCESS

While creativity and diversity of learning methods are important, those components alone can never produce life-changing impact on teachers and students. Small class groups by themselves are not a panacea. The class which will succeed is one led prayerfully and with a desire for juniors to be drawn to Christ. Whether in the teacher's devotional, in the discussion ideas suggested for the Scripture passage being studied, in the songs suggested to correlate with the Bible content, or in the conversation suggestions which help students apply Bible truth to their own lives, quality resources keep the attention focused on key spiritual issues for both teachers and students.

Henrietta Mears, the founder of Gospel Light Publications, used to tell children's workers about her own journey to faith in Jesus Christ: "First I learned to love my teacher, then I learned to love my teacher's God." From her own childhood experience of being drawn to Christ through the close, personal attention of a teacher who prayerfully loved a small group of children, Dr. Mears spearheaded the development of an extensive curriculum designed to help teachers effectively guide meaningful interaction with children.

BEHAVIOR CHALLENGES THROUGHOUT THE SESSION

PROBLEMS WHILE STUDENTS ARE ARRIVING

Tips for Preventing Problems

1. **Be ready before the kids arrive.** If you arrive at the last minute, kids will take advantage of the opportunity to start dismantling your room.

2. **Greet each student personally.** Individual attention conveys your interest in him or her as a person, not just as one of the bunch.

3. **Provide at least two activity options** from which to select. The act of making a choice gets students moving positively.

4. **Be enthusiastic** in everything you do and say. If you exude pleasure about teaching, kids will reflect pleasure in learning.

Tips for Resolving Problems

1. **Nonparticipation.** If a student announces, "I don't want to do that!" the best approach is a matter-of-fact response. "That's fine. It's OK to watch for awhile." After a few minutes, try inviting the student again to participate in a specific task. You may need to direct him or her to sit in a specific place while the activity is going on. It is usually not wise to allow a kid to just wander around the room, other than to allow a brief look at the available options.

2. **Shy Withdrawal.** Some juniors are shy or otherwise ill-at-ease at the start of a session. This is most common with visitors or those who attend irregularly. In many cases, the shy child simply withdraws further when fussed over. While it is important not to ignore the student, it is also important not to call attention to evidence of shyness.

3. **Pushing Limits.** It is not uncommon for juniors to "test" a teacher immediately upon arriving in the classroom. When this occurs, follow the same guidelines given below for resolving misbehavior.

WHILE JUNIORS ARE INVOLVED IN ACTIVITY

Tips for Preventing Problems

1. **Be prepared.** Juniors are likely to start misbehaving if you are unprepared with materials, or confused about instructions or procedures.

2. **Fit activities to group sizes.** Just because you can fit everyone around one giant table is not a good reason to do it. Juniors learn more and are better behaved in several small groups (up to eight students) than in one big group.

3. **Have a teacher participate** with each small group. Juniors still need the physical presence and participation of an adult to help them stay on task.

4. **Give clear directions**—and maybe a demonstration—of what the students are to do.

5. **Give appropriate recognition to kids** while they are doing what you want them to. Smiles, pats, winks and words of affirmation are potent allies in helping juniors do what is right.

Tips for Resolving Problems

1. **Misuse of materials.** Calmly and simply state why you cannot let the student continue to use objects in a way that could damage property or hurt people (e.g., "Those markers are needed for our art projects. I can't let you throw them."). If the misbehavior continues, either remove the materials or move the student.

2. **Aggression.** Juniors are quick to contend with each other. In many cases, verbal conflicts replace physical struggles. If you ask a student why he or she did something out of line, the usual response is to blame the other party. Instead, try this three-step approach:

    First, ask, "What happened?" or "What did you do?" If necessary, describe what you saw or heard, then ask, "What is your story?" The goal is not to fix blame and impose penalties; the goal is to show a better way to resolve differences.

    Second, ask, "Why is (hitting, pushing, etc.) not allowed?" Most juniors are perfectly capable of

(Continued on next page.)

telling why the action in question is a problem.

Third, lead the junior to correct the problem. Ask, "What can we do to make things better now?" In doing so, beware of forcing insincere apologies or of letting juniors think that saying "I'm sorry" absolves them of all responsibility.

3. **Clowning Around.** Occasionally juniors decide to be silly instead of fulfilling an activity's intended purpose. It is usually wise not to make a major issue out of such behavior. When possible, laugh along with them for a few moments. Once you have smiled together, then you can redirect them to the reason for the activity.

PROBLEMS WHILE JUNIORS SHOULD BE LISTENING

Tips for Preventing Problems

1. **Give plenty of opportunity for students to talk first.** Start each session with activities requiring interaction so juniors get to speak their piece before the time comes to focus more on listening.

2. **Remove distractions.** Juniors will pay attention better if their active eyes, ears and hands are not tantalized by a host of sights, sounds and objects.

3. **Have a teacher close to each student.** Juniors pay better attention and stay on task more consistently when an adult is part of their group.

Tips for Resolving Problems

1. **Talking out of turn.** Simply stop the junior who begins to talk out of turn with a gentle, "Excuse me, Summer. I know you want to talk, but right now it is time for you to listen. You'll have another turn to talk in a moment."

2. **Kids who dominate class discussions.** Juniors can accept the need to give everyone a chance to participate. The first person to respond to a question need not be the one to speak first. Request a signal (i.e., "thumbs up"). Requiring a signal allows you to be selective, sometimes calling on the slower, quieter, shyer person who may get "run over" by the more outgoing members of the group.

3. **Not paying attention.**

   a. Use the student's name. Drop it into your next sentence. A name is like a magnet, drawing the owner towards it.

   b. Move closer to the student. When you enter the student's space, the alerted junior will suddenly be aware of you.

   c. Touch the junior. A gentle touch on the shoulder, a pat on the head—they all send a clear signal to return.

   d. Change something. Talk a little faster or slower, softer or louder, stand up or sit down, lean forward or lean back. Do anything to change the rhythm of your words.

   e. Do something different. If more than one or two juniors are inattentive, you need to recapture the interest of the entire group. Try bringing your present activity to a quick end and start doing the next activity.

•

GUIDED CONVERSATION WITH PRETEENS

Guided conversation is an important way to help preteens learn at church. Guided conversation is informal discussion during classroom activities that directs students' thoughts, feelings and words toward the lesson focus. Think carefully about your conversation during classroom activities, because those moments are filled with the potential for meaningful learning. Be alert to ways of relating students' experiences to what God's Word says, thus helping students understand Bible truth.

Conversation with individuals and small groups also helps a teacher build a good relationship with each student. Juniors need to feel that you sincerely care for each of them and are interested in the things that interest them. As you guide the conversation, look for opportunities to express praise and encouragement. Each student needs to know that you recognize his or her honest efforts and the things he or she does well.

Your conversation with kids helps you discover what information a student knows (or doesn't know) about a particular topic. Engage juniors in a dialogue rather than a monologue. As juniors work on an activity, look for ways to make comments or ask questions to help them understand new words, ideas, Bible customs and facts they will encounter throughout the session.

Finally, guided conversation should stimulate—rather than interfere with—the student's learning experiences. The learning process is enhanced when you help the student relate Bible truths to his or her own experiences.

Think of ways you might tailor or build upon any conversation ideas in your curriculum to more specifically meet the needs of your own class. You will then be able to take advantage of those teachable moments that occur spontaneously during a session—opportunities that are uniquely yours.

HERE ARE SOME GUIDELINES FOR USING GUIDED CONVERSATION EFFECTIVELY.

1. Be prepared.
Read the information in your teacher's manual. Become familiar with the lesson focus. Review any conversation suggestions provided. Write several other questions you might ask. Keep these with you during the session.

2. Stay with your students as they work.
Kids need to know you are there, ready to listen and ready to talk.

3. Know the characteristics of the juniors you teach.
Be aware of individual differences in maturity. Be sensitive to each student's home situation and plan your conversation to include the variety of family situations represented in your class.

4. Recognize and accept the ways fifth and sixth graders respond to guided conversation.
Some juniors are quite verbal. Others may respond with nods or other motions.

5. Spend more time listening than you do talking.
Look directly at the student who is talking. Demonstrate your interest in what was said by responding to the specific ideas the student expressed.

The opportunities for guided conversation with juniors are endless. Prepare thoughtfully and prayerfully during the week. The Holy Spirit will use your words to reveal God's love and truth to your students.

LEADING A GOOD DISCUSSION

Teaching juniors requires a dialogue rather than a monologue. Teachers need to listen as much as—or more than—they speak. However, encouraging juniors to participate verbally is difficult for some teachers. The following questions are commonly asked about making a discussion truly productive, and not a "pooling of ignorance" or an unfocused, rambling conversation.

How do I keep preteens on track in a discussion?

Begin by preparing a few questions that will stimulate students' thinking. Limit the use of questions which require a student to recall information previously received. Knowledge questions ("What was Paul's occupation?") do not stimulate interest in the discussion because once the question has been answered, little more can be said. Asking too many knowledge questions can stifle interest and decrease participation of those kids who lack Bible knowledge or confidence in their abilities.

Instead, ask comprehension questions to help students explore the meaning of information. For example, questions such as "What do you think was the hardest part about Paul's work?" require students to think before they respond. Because comprehension questions do not require "right answers," they encourage discussion rather than limit it. In fact, each student may suggest a different answer to the question, thus increasing the opportunity for discussion, while keeping the students on track.

Also ask application questions to focus thinking on students' personal situations. For example, "When have you felt like Paul must have felt when he was falsely accused?" When Bible truth begins touching a student's daily life, the student will be interested.

How do I get them back on track if a digression occurs?

First, decide whether the lesson topic is really more important than the digression. If students show a significant interest in whatever drew the group off track, and if you feel that topic has real value to the group, and if you feel capable of guiding the group in learning about the new topic, then you may decide to leave your lesson plan and stay with the new issue.

However, if the digression does not warrant a complete change of direction, use questions again to bring attention back to the topic and its particular implications. You may restate the original question to remind students of the issue at hand. Or try rephrasing the question if students' comments indicate they did not understand what you asked them. Or move on to a new question if you feel the students have probably said all they are likely to contribute to the previous question.

It is usually helpful to acknowledge that the group has been off on a tan-

gent. Avoid making a big deal out of it, but be clear that it is time to return to the session topic. A sense of humor at such times will certainly help you avoid a developing power struggle with students.

How do I handle interruptions?

If no one else seems distracted by the interruption, just keep on going. Remember, juniors tend to be used to situations where several things are going on at once, and a minimal interruption may almost pass unnoticed by everyone else but you.

If the interruption definitely caught the class's attention, acknowledge it as matter-of-factly as possible, then restate the question being discussed. You may also want to summarize some of the key points already made in the discussion.

How do I know if kids are bored with a discussion, and what should I do about it if they are?

You will never need to wonder if juniors are bored. They will make it very clear, either by announcing loudly, "This is boring!" or by "cutting up" and causing trouble in some fashion. What to do about a boring discussion is another matter.

It is usually best to assume that once boredom has taken hold in a discussion, it is a terminal condition. It is easier to recapture interest with a dif-

(Continued on next page.)

(Continued from previous page.)

ferent activity (i.e., the next thing you had planned to do), than rejuvenate interest in the same discussion.

What do I do when no one says anything?

If you've asked a thought-provoking question, assume that students need at least a few moments to think. Rather than getting nervous when your question is greeted by silence, simply say, "I don't want to hear the first idea that pops into your head. Take a few moments and think about it." Then be silent for a bit (no more than 20-30 seconds), and repeat or rephrase the question. If you still get no response, award yourself 50 points for "Stumping the Experts!" or "Asking a Question No One Has an Answer For!" or some such category. Then give your own answer to the question and move on.

If your students' reluctance to discuss is a recurring problem, take a good look at the questions you have been asking. Are they too vague? Are they threatening? Do they require knowledge the students do not have? Are the answers too obvious?

If the questions are fine, evaluate your response to what the students do say. Are you unwilling to accept students and their answers if they differ from the "correct" responses? Do you have a tendency to always "improve" the students' answers? Work at creating a climate of openness.

Finally, add some variety to your approach in asking questions:

- Have students write their answers on paper. This allows them time to organize their thoughts. Then invite them to read what they wrote.
- Divide the class into smaller groups. You may ask all groups the same questions, or assign different questions to each group. Then invite volunteers to share the answers for their groups.

What do I do when kids are only giving "pat" answers?

Try the same ideas suggested when students do not answer at all. The root problem is often the same in either case: The students do not feel secure sharing what they really think.

CLASSROOMS THAT AID LEARNING

A classroom is a silent partner that has the potential to aid or hinder student learning, to enhance or distract from even the best curriculum and teaching methods. Classrooms for fifth and sixth graders need to reflect order, friendliness and space for a variety of learning experiences. Consciously or unconsciously, teachers and students are influenced by their classroom environment.

When the students are actively involved in the learning process, there needs to be adequate space for games, dramas, etc. Tables and chairs should be portable so they can be pushed aside, creating a large open area in the classroom.

YOUR EQUIPMENT

Appropriately sized furnishings are important if the child is to be comfortable and able to learn efficiently. The height (floor to chair seat) for chairs should be 14-16 inches (35-40 cm). Tables should be 10 inches (25 cm) above chair seat height.

Survey the furnishings in your classroom. If they are too small or too large, exchange furniture with another department so that all benefit. If this exchange is not feasible, ask a carpenter in your church to adjust chairs and tables to correct heights. Painting and repairing furnishings can be done with the combined efforts of parents and teachers.

YOUR ROOM

From the time a student enters your classroom, the surroundings affect that student's attitude and resulting learning. The effect may be positive or negative. Look at the room from the perspective of your students. Consider these questions:

1. How do you feel about entering the room? Do you want to come in?

2. Is the room neat and clean? Does the air smell fresh?

3. Is the room colorful and light?

4. Is there something in the room that is particularly attractive to you? What have you contributed to the room's decorations—bulletin board, displays, photos, posters, etc.?

5. Do you feel encouraged to become involved in an activity, or is everything so sterile you are reluctant to touch anything?

6. Are there windows you can easily see through?

7. Can you find and return the materials you need?

8. Is there space enough to move around without bumping into furniture?

9. Are the bulletin boards and chalkboards at your eye level? Does the material displayed on the boards encourage Bible learning?

As you answer these questions, list the things you want to change in your room. Determine which of the adjustments you can do with little or no help. Then accomplish these as money, time, materials and space become available. Work around those things you cannot change.

If other groups use the room during the week, provide a room set-up sketch for your custodian so the major furnishings can be properly arranged each week.

SHARiNG YOUR CLASSROOM SPACE

◆ At the beginning of the school year, meet with the teacher(s) with whom you share a classroom. Talk about the needs of each program and make specific plans about how to help each other. Come to an agreement on the best arrangement of furniture and equipment. Plan to remove any furnishings or supplies not in use by either program. If possible, try to have the same age groups using the same rooms. Plan a system of ongoing communication.

◆ If the classroom will be used by students of the same age, plan to share equipment and as many supplies as possible. Make decisions ahead of time about the use of the shared equipment. What can be placed on the walls or bulletin boards? When

are the wastebaskets to be emptied? How much cleanup must be done by teachers and what can the custodial staff be expected to do? What should be done with materials accidentally left in the classroom?

◆ If you have a problem with materials disappearing, locked storage space should be requested for your classroom. If locked storage space in the classroom is limited, purchase some sturdy cardboard file boxes. Label each one with the type of material it contains. Then, either store the cartons in another room in the building where they will not be disturbed, or arrange for teachers to bring them to each session.

◆ Consider using portable storage carts. Carts can be purchased or

built. When the materials on the cart are not being used, the cart may be kept in a central supply room.

◆ If sharing bulletin boards is a problem, either assign each board for use by a different class, or build reversible bulletin boards. Another option is to make a portable bulletin board (fiberboard covered with fabric) which can be hung over a permanent board.

◆ Open shelves on wheels can be turned to the wall when not in use.

◆ If a custodian's help is available, give him or her clear diagrams for the room arrangements for each class.

BOYS AND GIRLS: ARE THEY COMPATIBLE?

"Oh no! Here they come!" a sixth-grade girl groans as two boys approach the classroom. But a huge smile lights up her face as she says the words.

"Eew-w! You've got cooties!" Generations of fifth- and sixth-grade boys and girls have accused each other of being infested with these small, invisible, insects.

The years before the onset of adolescence seem to be when young people are most openly antagonistic towards peers of the opposite sex. Some of the tension between girls and boys is the result of a growing self-awareness and sexual identity. And some is the result of anxiety over a growing awareness of and curiosity about gender differences.

The typical pattern of at least occasional conflict poses challenges for the teacher of fifth and sixth graders.

CHALLENGES

◆ Boys and girls may resist sitting next to or working with members of the opposite sex.

◆ Many girls and boys have significantly different interests and preferred ways of interacting.

◆ As adolescence approaches, girls tend to mature more rapidly than boys. A group with both fifth and sixth graders is likely to have noticeable differences in maturity levels between older girls and younger boys.

◆ Verbal put-downs of each other are common ways to cover nervousness and attraction.

◆ Both boys and girls at this age tend to be intolerant of those who are different from them.

Some teachers choose "the path of least resistance," and completely separate girls and boys. However, same-sex groups have their own set of problems:

◆ Another set of challenges (i.e., a group of boys getting "wild;" a group of girls getting silly) can be at least as hard to deal with as those faced in a combined-sex group;

◆ Certain "chemical combinations" (two or more kids who are great as individuals, but "real trouble" when they are together) are more likely to combust without the mediating influence of the other gender;

◆ Kids do not learn to get along with the other sex;

◆ Kids are likely to miss out on positive relationships with adults of both sexes. With so many children being raised in single-parent homes, preteens need the opportunity to be part of a group guided by both women and men.

Consider the following suggestions to minimize the above challenges while helping girls and boys learn to accept and appreciate each other.

TIPS

1. Plan ways to mix boys and girls in small-group activities.

If you tell a fifth-grade boy to sit next to a sixth-grade girl, or vice versa, you are likely to hear vociferous protests. Instead, invite both girls and boys to get involved in an interesting activity. When children enjoy being busily occupied, they are unlikely to create a fuss over who happens to be working alongside. Or simply state that "Just for now you need to be in this group. Later you can choose who you work with."

2. Minimize competition between the sexes.

Fifth and sixth graders do love contests and games (as long as they seem to win more than they lose). Also, a great deal of energy can be generated by challenging the girls to outdo boys and encouraging the boys to best the girls. However, be sparing and cautious with such competitive endeavors, for they contribute to an "us versus them" attitude, rather than fostering acceptance and cooperation.

3. Provide both male and female role models.

Boys and girls need positive relationships with both men and women who respect and support each other. If your teaching staff is all male or female, regularly involve other adults in your class sessions. Consider these suggestions for ways to involve guests:

• Interview guests about interesting life experiences.

• Ask guests to serve a snack.

• Enlist a guest's help with an activity.

• Ask a guest to present a special talent (music, dramatic reading, photography, art, cooking, etc.).

4. Keep your sense of humor.

Rather than being offended when a fifth or sixth grader says something derogatory about "yucky boys" or "gross girls," keep the atmosphere light. Simply laugh and say, "Oh, right! You really hate boys, Renee." Another way to do this is to comment on your own appreciation for people of both sexes: "I used to say stuff like that when I was your age, but then I learned that girls are really terrific!" Your positive example, and your acceptance of all students, will go a long way towards building healthy attitudes between boys and girls.

THE LEADER'S ROLE

The following guidelines summarize the basic tasks involved in supporting and building successful teaching teams.

BASIC FUNCTION

Prayerfully build relationships with both teachers and students in order to ensure effective Bible learning.

NOTE: In a department with just two teachers, the leader responsibilities may be informally shared. When three or more people are on the team, one person should be designated as Lead Teacher or Department Leader.

CLASS RESPONSIBILITIES

◆ Coordinate teacher tasks, including use of supplies and room setup.

◆ Greet students as they arrive and help them become involved in an activity.

◆ Assist teachers as needed (e.g., discipline, activity completion, etc.), maintaining the time schedule for the session.

NOTE: In smaller departments, the leader may guide an activity or class group. In larger departments (18 or more students), it is best if the leader is free to move among the activities being led by teachers.

◆ Observe, affirm and evaluate teachers at work in order to note strengths to encourage and areas where improvement is possible.

TEAM RESPONSIBILITIES

◆ Pray regularly for others on your teaching team.

◆ Work with your church leadership to identify and enlist qualified people to join your teaching team.

◆ Consistently affirm teachers for their efforts and faithfulness.

◆ Seek to improve the effectiveness of your teaching team by leading regular training/planning meetings which provide opportunities for spiritual growth and development of teaching skills.

◆ Encourage teachers in their out-of-class efforts to build relationships with students and their families, focusing on follow-up strategies for visitors and absentees.

◆ Channel communications between church leadership and your teaching team.

THE TEACHER'S ROLE

The following guidelines summarize the basic tasks involved in nurturing the spiritual growth of juniors.

BASIC FUNCTION

Prayerfully build relationships with students in order to guide and involve them in life-changing Bible learning.

CLASS RESPONSIBILITIES

◆ Arrange materials and room to create an effective learning environment.

◆ Greet each student upon arrival and engage him or her in conversation and meaningful activity.

◆ Model the love of Christ and the power of God's Word and the Holy Spirit to each student.

◆ Show love and concern for students by getting to know them, accepting them as they are, actively listening to them and sharing their concerns, needs, and joys.

◆ Affirm and support students for specific evidences of growth and learning.

◆ Guide Bible learning by:
  • being well-prepared to use Bible stories, verses/passages, questions and comments in order to accomplish the lesson aims;
  • connecting Bible content to needs and interests;
  • selecting challenging learning activities;
  • encouraging students to be honest in expressing their ideas and feelings;
  • helping students explore and apply Bible truths to achieve understanding and lead to changes in attitude and behavior.

◆ Participate with students in Bible study, learning activities and in prayer times.

OUT-OF-CLASS RESPONSIBILITIES

◆ Pray regularly for each student.
◆ Cultivate the friendship and interests of students and their families, seeking to win unchurched families to Christ and the church.

◆ Show love and concern by following up on visitors and absentees.

TEAM RESPONSIBILITIES

◆ Pray regularly for others on your teaching team.

◆ Seek to identify and recommend people to join your teaching team.

◆ Improve the effectiveness of your teaching team by participating regularly in training/planning meetings.

NOTE: Just as Jesus sent His followers out in pairs, and to meet the variety of needs and interests in any group of children, all teachers should serve on teams so at least two teachers are in the room at all times. This staffing also ensures a responsible person is available in case an emergency arises, and provides protection for the teachers should any question ever be raised about how children are being treated.

HOW JUNIORS LEARN BEST

There are some natural differences in the ways different people learn, and preteens are no exception. Each child has his or her unique approach to gaining knowledge and skill. Just as no two students swing a baseball bat or skate in exactly the same way, there is a wide spectrum of approaches to learning. Anyone who desires to teach juniors needs to keep this diversity in mind.

Fortunately, there are some major approaches to learning which all juniors share in common. While a fifth grader may lack some of the skills used by a sixth grader, and while a child who loves to read may approach learning differently from a child who prefers solving puzzles, consider these five major features which help all juniors learn at their optimum levels.

1. RELATIONSHIPS POWERFULLY IMPACT LEARNING.

Juniors are more powerfully influenced by persons than by any other factor in a learning environment. The way a child moves, thinks, feels, values and believes are all patterned after people he or she loves, trusts and admires. Even though fifth and sixth graders spend huge quantities of time in front of television sets, the relationships they have with live people in their families, neighborhoods and schools are the dominant motivators in their lives.

Therefore: Spend time with juniors. The teacher who makes a lasting impact on juniors is the one who makes good use of time spent with them. The key to quality time with juniors is to give focused attention to each student. Juniors respond best when they feel someone is talking personally to them, listening attentively to them, caring individually for them.

2. EXAMPLES TEACH MORE THAN WORDS.

Relationships are so important because preteens are more strongly influenced by examples than by words. Teachers who build positive relationships with juniors become powerful examples the students want to be like. At an age when kids are starting to look outside the family for role models, a caring, friendly teacher is in a critical position to be someone the child will imitate. However, if a teacher is only observed doing "teacher things" such as telling stories, reading aloud, writing on the chalkboard, holding visual aids, etc., there is not much behavior the student can reflect.

Therefore: Demonstrate what you want juniors to mimic. If you want your students to memorize Bible verses, get busy and memorize along with them. If you want them to bring their Bibles to class, bring yours. If you want students to pray for the needs of others, ask students to tell their prayer requests and pray for them.

3. MEANINGFUL ACTIVITY PROMOTES INTEREST AND APPLICATION.

While preteens are innately curious, they are not always interested in the things we are ready to present to them. The most effective category of interest-grabbing approaches is simply to give fifth and sixth graders something worthwhile to do.

Keep in mind that juniors not only learn by what they do, *they literally learn what it is they do.* A student may listen to instructions about being kind; he or she may hear ideas of specific ways to be kind. But only the student who does a kind act is actually learning to be kind. Sadly, in many classes,

(Continued on next page.)

(Continued from previous page.)

students have learned mostly to listen to people talk about Christianity. While listening to information is an important part of the learning process, we must not delude ourselves into equating listening with learning.

Therefore: Plan activities that practice what you teach. While almost any activity may be used to teach about almost any topic, choose the activity closest to the life application you want the student to make. Making banners about kindness may stimulate juniors to think about being kind, but application becomes tangible only when a student actually practices kindness. Choose activities based more on the process the student goes through than the product which results.

4. QUESTIONS STIMULATE THINKING.

Many moments of high interest are created by a thoughtful question. The average teacher asks questions to find out what kids already know. The excellent teacher asks questions to stimulate kids to learn something new.

Therefore: Ask open-ended questions. You arouse curiosity when you ask juniors for their opinions, feelings, and ideas. These open-ended, what-do-you-think? questions do not limit students to one single correct answer. They encourage participation, since many students can share insights about the same question.

Also ask questions which prod juniors to think about how truth is put into practice in daily living. Application questions usually ask students to think of a specific way to do something that has been learned.

5. EACH STUDENT HAS A UNIQUE LEARNING STYLE.

Each student learns at a pace and with a style that is unique. Some need a quiet corner to concentrate, while others prefer having music or other background noise while reading or listening. Some learn best by starting with the "big picture," while others require moving through one concept at a time. Some learn well from spoken or written words, others need something visual. Because of each student's individual bent, no single instructional approach is effective with everyone.

Therefore: Provide variety and choices. Give each student the opportunity for balanced learning. Learning improves when students are taught in ways that fit their individual needs and interests. In most cases, students' preferences are valid indicators of their strengths. Thus, give juniors opportunity to make some choices about what to do during a session.

THE TEACHING-LEARNING PROCESS

Ministry to fifth- and sixth-grade students is enhanced when we understand and plan experiences to meet the following basic steps in a student's learning process.

1. LISTENING

An essential and basic learning task is listening or giving attention. The teacher seeking to initiate the learning process must first get the attention of juniors. Gaining interest often involves motivating the student through both the room environment and student activities which introduce the material to be studied. The moment when a student arrives is a key time in hooking his or her interest into the lesson for the day. Games, experiments and skits are some good ways to attract a junior's attention.

2. EXPLORING

The second step in the learning process—exploring—involves the careful investigation of a problem or subject. The student needs to become an explorer, involved in the search for something not yet known or experienced. He is not a passive listener or mere spectator, but a central and active participant. Much of the exploration juniors need to do involves using the Bible or other study aids. Exploration may also involve posing questions, defining problems or suggesting possible approaches to dealing with life situations.

3. DISCOVERING

As a result of the listening and exploring processes, the student discovers for him- or herself what the Bible says. Then, guided by the Holy Spirit, the student understands the Bible's impli-

cations for his or her own life.

Discovering God's eternal truths in His Word is an exciting process. Too often the teacher is the only one who makes these discoveries. Although the teacher may excitedly share them with the students, why shouldn't the joy of discovery also be the student's as he or she is guided by a skilled teacher? Time constraints may limit how many discoveries juniors can make during a session, but time should not be an excuse for simply trying to "cover the material" without involving juniors in the process. The goal is to have juniors learn and apply Bible truth, not "cover the material."

4. APPROPRIATING

Once the student has discovered the meaning of the Bible passage, he or she needs to think in a personal way about the truths involved. The student must relate the meanings and values discovered to his or her own experiences. Bible knowledge that is not being examined for personal implications is not accomplishing its God-intended purpose.

Guide the student's task of appropriating, or making Bible truth his or her own. Ask students to describe situations which need to be solved on the basis of biblical truth. Then ask, "What would you do in this situation? What does the Bible passage tell us about dealing with situations like these?"

Personally appropriating the Bible truth of a particular lesson enables the student to recognize its meaning for his or her own feelings and behavior. As a result of this step in the learning process, the student knows what God expects of him or her in situations related to this truth.

5. ASSUMING RESPONSIBILITY

This is the crown of the learning process, the place where the previous tasks—listening, exploring, discovering and appropriating—culminate. Here God's truth actually changes and molds a student's thinking, attitude and behavior. For it is at this point that our efforts to communicate God's truth should result in changed lives. Our juniors must be led to actually do certain things on the basis of what they have been experiencing (in the previous steps of the learning process).

The true test of learning comes when a student voluntarily uses what he or she has learned in new situations. This may involve practicing a quality of behavior in the middle of class activities (settling a disagreement in a friendly way, cooperating with others in a group project, etc.). It may also involve planning service projects or other opportunities to put Bible learning into action. At other times, it may be best to have students plan specific actions to take during the coming week.

The process of human understanding and learning is summed up in these steps to learning. Listening, exploring, discovering, appropriating and assuming responsibility are not simply activities in which students are to be engaged, but are inseparably bound together with Christian teaching/learning goals and objectives.

Through the Holy Spirit's guidance of a thoughtful teacher, the spiritual dimension of a student's personality can continue its growth and development.

LEARNING ACTIVITIES— WHAT ARE THEY?

Learning activities are creative activities designed to involve students. These hands-on activities may involve games, art, music, writing, drama or service projects. But each learning activity is more than just action for the sake of action. What qualifies an activity for use at Sunday School? How can we be certain that the activity will result in Bible learning? When does an activity become a learning activity?

Here are some questions to ask as you plan effective learning activities for your class:

Question 1: How does the activity introduce, teach or review a Bible truth? What helpful questions and comments can you say to connect the activity with Bible truth?

Question 2: In what ways does the activity help build relationships among students?

Question 3: How does the activity give students the opportunity to relate Bible truth to their everyday experiences?

BE SPECIFIC, YET FLEXIBLE

Each learning activity must be specific enough to permit the child to feel assured (as the activity develops) that the activity has purpose. However, it must be flexible enough to take into account the ability and skill level of each student.

For example, as a teacher prepares for a learning activity in which skits will be used to dramatize a Bible story, that teacher will make sure the activity includes both academic and nonacademic-oriented tasks (reading the scripts as well as making and using props or backdrops). A teacher also will offer juniors opportunities to participate in planning. Often a student's ideas help make the activity

more effective than if only the plans of the teacher were used.

HOW TO GUIDE ACTIVITIES

Five main steps are needed for learning to take place in an activity:

1. Introduce the purpose of each activity.

When an activity is first presented to juniors, it is important to explain *why* the students will be doing it, and not simply *what* they will do. For example, kids may choose an art activity because they like to draw cartoons. Help them see beyond the procedures to the purpose: e.g., "to help us learn ways to trust God in hard times."

2. Involve juniors in Bible skills.

Activities need to include time for students to review or gather some specific Bible information. Choose methods that are compatible with students' abilities and interests. For example, some students may simply read Bible words the teacher has lettered on a chalkboard, while others will locate and read the verses in the Bible. A student who likes to read might use a Bible dictionary, concordance or encyclopedia.

3. Guide the conversation to emphasize the purpose of the activity.

As juniors work on an activity, the teacher uses informal conversation to guide a child's thoughts, feelings and words toward the lesson focus. For example, as a game activity begins to lose focus, the teacher might ask one of the players, "What are some other things you might say in this situation in order to show compassion, like our Bible passage says?"

By being alert to relate the student's experience to what God's Word says, a teacher helps that student understand Bible truth. Informal con-

versation is most effective when students are in groups of no more than eight students with a teacher.

4. Lead students to identify what they are learning by doing the activity.

As juniors near the completion of an activity, the teacher should ask them to put into words what they have learned about the main truth of the lesson: "What have you learned today about what to do when you've made a wrong choice?" "What information did you discover about the way in which Solomon made choices?" When students find such a question difficult to answer, the teacher knows that more learning is needed.

5. Lead juniors in sharing with others what they learned.

One of the most important steps in the learning process is sharing with someone else what was learned.

• Asking the student to think of what to tell someone else about an activity is a helpful way to lead the student to think of the point of a lesson. "If you were to tell a friend about this activity, how would you explain what you've learned about settling arguments?"

• Give juniors an opportunity to share their learning activities with those in other groups. This sharing of activities can be done in a variety of ways: Students can show what they did while the teacher explains it; the teacher can ask questions to lead juniors in explaining what they learned; a few kids can speak on behalf of the rest of their group; each group member can offer one or two sentences to tell the most important (or interesting) thing he or she learned.

• Occasionally you may arrange for a group of students to display and explain their activity to children in a different age level.

ART

Learning activities involving creative art experiences provide an enjoyable and effective way for fifth and sixth graders to express what they have learned and to plan ways to put that learning into action. As you use art activities, remember that the learning process is more important than the end product. As you select and use art experiences, focus the student's attention on the Bible truth concerned, not on the result or quality of the work.

For example:

◆ As a student works to illustrate a situation in his or her life, the teacher should ask questions to stimulate the student to think about the action being shown.

"What happened just before the scene you are making?"

"Which person in this scene is a good example to follow? Why?"

The teacher should also ask questions to help the student focus on the main truth illustrated in a story or Bible passage.

"What did you learn about success from these verses?"

"What could you do this week that would show love and faithfulness to God as David did?"

◆ As a student draws, paints or models a contemporary scene, the teacher should connect this familiar experience to a Bible story or Bible passage.

"What are you doing in this picture that is the same as what David did in our story? "How would it help the person in your picture if he or she remembered the words of Proverbs 3:3-6?"

BENEFITS OF ART ACTIVITIES

Lesson-related art activities can help a student

◆ show in a concrete way an abstract concept such as following God's wisdom, forgiving others, depending on God, serving others;

◆ think in terms of specific actions (what to do when feeling jealous, how to express anger) as he or she applies a Bible verse such as "Do not let any unwholesome talk come out of your mouths, but only what is helpful for building others up" (Ephesians 4:29);

◆ show new discoveries (for example, illustrating the meaning of key words in a Bible passage);

◆ put into practice Bible truths (for example, making posters to encourage others in the church family to participate in a giving project);

◆ express thoughts that may be difficult to put into words (such as drawing a cartoon about a way to show forgiveness to someone).

TIPS FOR LEADING ART ACTIVITIES

◆ Before juniors begin using the art materials, ask each one to tell his or her idea for a picture, scene, etc.

◆ If an activity requires use of a material which is new to you, or if the activity involves several steps, make a sample before class.

◆ Materials for art activities are limited only by your imagination. Enlist the help of interested parents and church members in collecting and labeling items. List the articles you need in your church newsletter or bulletin.

◆ Store materials and equipment in an organized way where students can see and reach them. Label containers and shelves so students can easily return items to their proper places.

◆ You may want to cover tables with plastic tablecloths or newspapers in order to make cleanup easy.

◆ Keep paper towels or sponges handy so cleanup will be easy when a spill occurs.

◆ Occasionally provide a new material for students to use in working on art activities. Juniors who may usually be uninterested in art projects will be motivated to participate with the addition of spray glitter, or metallic or neon pens.

◆ Some juniors are self-conscious about their artistic abilities. Help students feel comfortable by grouping several students together to complete an art project. Then each student may participate in a different way, suggesting ideas, organizing supplies, drawing, etc.

CREATIVE WRITING

Creative writing activities can provide valuable learning experiences for juniors when the experiences are planned according to the abilities of the students, and when they hold no threat of failure. Committing thoughts to paper—as a poem, a story, a journal, a paraphrase of a Bible verse, etc.—aids a student in recalling and then developing the key thoughts expressed.

For example:

◆ A student who writes a letter to a friend explaining the main point of the lesson is developing skill in sharing the student's faith with others.

◆ A student who rewrites a Bible verse in his or her own words is grappling with meaning, not just rote memory.

◆ A student who contributes a word or phrase to a group composition is encouraged to feel a part of the class and enjoys the success of having his or her ideas accepted.

BENEFITS OF CREATIVE WRITING ACTIVITIES

Lesson-related creative writing activities can help juniors:

◆ list/describe specific concrete examples of an abstract concept such as how to be like "good soil" in accepting God's Word, how to handle failure, what it means to be successful in God's eyes;

◆ express their feelings about God, or about their experiences and needs;

◆ synthesize their thinking as they put ideas into words;

◆ record ways they put Bible truths into practice in daily life;

◆ show love to others (for example, writing letters or advice columns to be included in a church newsletter, writing and recording Bible stories to be given to a preschool class, etc.).

TIPS FOR LEADING WRITING ACTIVITIES

◆ Write on chalkboard or scratch paper any words that juniors need to know how to spell.

◆ Let a student who doesn't enjoy writing record his or her ideas on tape. Later, write or type these ideas and add them to the project being worked on.

◆ Let juniors work together, making sure one person in the group is skilled enough to write the ideas of the group.

◆ A student's creative writing efforts are usually more productive when the teacher has done some "pump priming" to stimulate thinking.

◆ Show and discuss pictures or objects to get ideas flowing.

◆ Provide "story starters" (partially described situations which kids build on or complete).

◆ Suggest a problem for students to solve.

◆ Before juniors begin writing, encourage them to talk about possible ideas they might use.

DRAMA

Drama activities such as skits, puppets, pantomime, etc. are valuable learning opportunities because of the process the student experiences, not because of the quality of the final performance. Bible stories come alive when juniors act them out, and Bible truth is seen to be relevant when applied to contemporary situations.

BENEFITS OF DRAMA ACTIVITIES

◆ A student portraying a Bible character will clearly recall what that person said and did.

◆ A student speaking through a puppet may express thoughts and feelings that would not likely be spoken otherwise.

◆ Planning and then acting out a situation will push juniors to think about the application of Bible truth to a real-life circumstance.

◆ Dramatic activities provide a unique opportunity to briefly step into another person's shoes and experience some of his or her attitudes and feelings.

◆ Acting out specific examples of friendliness, faithfulness to God and ways to show integrity gives concrete meaning to these otherwise abstract words.

TIPS FOR LEADING DRAMA ACTIVITIES

◆ A good way to introduce drama in your class is to begin by reading the Bible story narration while class members pantomime the appropriate action. Later, students may read dialogue parts in the story.

◆ If possible, provide a box of costumes and simple props to help stimulate students' thinking.

◆ Plan for an area in your room that can be cleared of furnishings and used as a stage for the dramatization.

◆ If juniors feel unsure of themselves, they will sometimes try to cover up their insecurity by acting silly. To prevent this,

• start with very simple stories/situations with a minimum of dialogue;

• talk over the story/situation in enough detail so juniors feel sure of what to do;

• demonstrate how a specific part or action might be acted out or pantomimed (or let a volunteer do this), then let several juniors show how they would do it;

• if a student pauses during the drama, ask a question to help him or her remember the action of the story or think of what to do next;

• don't force a student to act out a story or situation, but do involve him or her in other ways—planning, evaluating, prop-making, etc.; encourage participation by suggesting that a shy student take a part with little or no speaking;

• when presenting role-plays of contemporary situations, provide several alternatives of ways a character might respond to the problem presented, allowing juniors to choose the option they feel best illustrates the concept being taught.

HELPFUL HINTS FOR USING SCRIPTS IN CLASS

Prepare.

◆ Purchase several highlighter pens for students to use in marking their parts.

◆ Read the script, noting any vocabulary or pronunciation help you will need to give your students.

Vary the script presentation.

◆ Have the entire group read through the skit in pairs or small groups before presenting the skit to the whole group.

◆ Give everyone in the group a script to follow as selected readers read aloud.

◆ Ask volunteers to pantomime actions as others read the script aloud.

◆ Assign parts to small groups to read in unison.

For even more dramatic impact,

◆ give scripts to students ahead of time (or to early arrivals, or even during the week before class) to practice their lines;

◆ occasionally ask parent or teen helpers to perform a script for your class;

◆ plan to read a part requiring significant dramatic expression yourself.

GAMES

Play and learn! Often juniors are not aware of the direct learning value of a game, but they participate enthusiastically because they enjoy the game. Bible games are helpful tools for involving juniors in an enjoyable way to discover, use and remember Bible truths and passages.

For example:

◆ Writing key words of a Bible passage and their definitions on index cards to use in a relay game can give the teacher opportunities to ask juniors to tell of times they do or do not show the quality of the word they defined.

◆ Playing a game similar to tic-tac-toe in which students draw pictures of contemporary situations in each section of the game board can lead juniors to think of ways to put God's Word into practice.

◆ Flipping coins onto a grid of discussion-starter cards can help juniors respond to real life situations.

BENEFITS OF BIBLE GAMES

Through Bible games the student can
◆ discover new information,
◆ review Bible truths,
◆ develop skill in using the Bible,
◆ apply Bible truths,
◆ memorize Bible passages,
◆ increase his or her skill in interacting in a group situation (cooperating, being fair and honest).

TIPS FOR LEADING GAMES

1. **Explain rules clearly and simply.** It's helpful to write the rules to the game. Make sure you explain rules step by step.

2. **Offer a practice round.** When playing a game for the first time with your class, play it a few times just for practice. Juniors will learn the rules best by actually playing the game.

3. **Choose games appropriate to the skill level of your class.** If you know that some students in your class are not able to read or write as well as others, avoid playing games that depend solely on those skills for success. When playing a game in which students must answer questions, suggest that the student whose turn it is may answer the question or ask a member of his or her team to answer the question.

4. **Vary the process by which teams are formed.** Allow students to group themselves into teams of three or four members each. Play the game one time. Then announce that the person on each team who is wearing the most (red) should rotate to another team. Then play the game again. As you repeat this rotation process, vary the method of rotation so that students play with several different juniors each time. Keep in mind that grouping several boys and girls together in one team can often help prevent active games from becoming too rowdy.

Music

Music is often used with fifth and sixth graders as merely something to do until all the latecomers arrive, or as a change of pace from the real learning that is going on in the session. Such limited use of music misses the powerful impact music can have on juniors' understanding, their memory and application of Bible truth. While music is always an important ingredient in the worship segment of a session, it can also help students in learning and applying Bible truths.

For example:

◆ A group may learn a new song in order to sing it for others in the church, telling what they have learned about Bible truth through the words of the song.

◆ A group may develop motions to the song's words that will help them understand and recall the words of Scripture.

◆ A group may combine art and music by illustrating the words and meaning of a song.

◆ Juniors can identify times during the coming week when it would be helpful for them to remember a song they have learned to sing, or have illustrated, or have accompanied with instruments.

Benefits of Music Activities

A learning activity involving music is an enjoyable way for juniors to be actively involved in learning and remembering scriptural truths. Music carefully selected for a specific purpose can help a student:

◆ learn Bible truths or doctrine,

◆ memorize Bible passages,

◆ remember to display Christian conduct,

◆ feel an atmosphere of quietness and worship,

◆ move smoothly from one activity to another,

◆ relax.

Tips for Leading Music Learning Activities

◆ Ask the following six questions about any song you intend to use:
  1. Is the meaning obvious to juniors?
  2. Is it easy to sing?
  3. Does the song relate to the current unit of Bible lessons?
  4. Are the words scripturally and doctrinally correct?
  5. Does the song build positive attitudes?
  6. Will juniors enjoy it?

◆ Invite a member of your church's choir or worship team, or a parent who is musically skilled, to lead a music activity during one or more lessons.

◆ Use the music cassette provided with your curriculum to help you become familiar with a song.

◆ Ask a student in your class to bring an electronic keyboard to class to accompany a song.

SERVICE PROJECTS

Service projects allow a teacher to take a class beyond simply hearing about obeying God, talking about obeying God and even planning ways of obeying God. Acts of service done as part of a group are effective ways to help juniors actually begin obeying God by assisting others.

◆ A class may do an art, drama or music activity in order to benefit another class or group.

For example:

- Display posters or banners in hallways to encourage positive actions and attitudes.
- Make theme-related centerpieces for a church dinner or luncheon.
- Present a Bible story skit for an adult class.

◆ Juniors may work together to care for church facilities (pick up litter, pull weeds, clean closets, sort pictures, etc.).

◆ Students may plan a class party to which they invite nonchurched friends.

◆ Juniors may enjoy adopting a "grandparent" in a rest home, or a missionary child their same age, or a child in a children's hospital.

◆ Students may collect canned foods, outgrown clothing, slightly used books and games to donate to a local missions organization.

◆ Preteens can assist in a worship service by handing out bulletins, receiving the offering, reading Scripture, etc.

◆ Volunteer your class to serve at a special event by setting up or taking down chairs and tables, serving beverages at a dinner or luncheon.

BENEFITS OF SERVICE PROJECT ACTIVITIES

Service projects that grow out of Bible lessons can help juniors:

◆ encourage one another to do what God's Word teaches,

◆ experience the joy of giving to others,

◆ accept responsibility to complete a task,

◆ learn to work together,

◆ recognize that God's Word leads His people to action.

TIPS FOR INVOLVING JUNIORS IN SERVICE PROJECTS

◆ Plan ahead to be sure your project is more than "busy work." Clearly explain to kids how their work will benefit others. If possible, allow time for kids to brainstorm ideas to help others.

◆ If the service project will last more than a week or two, consider making a chart or poster on which to record your progress.

◆ Invite someone from the group that will benefit from the project to your class. Have students interview this person to learn about the needs they will be helping to meet.

◆ Involve parents or responsible teens to assist in supervising juniors as they work on their project.

◆ Take pictures (photographs or videos) of kids as they pull weeds, sort pictures, deliver canned goods, etc. Then display the photos in your classroom or show the video during a future class session.

MISSIONS PROJECTS

Fifth and sixth graders are intensely curious about the world and its great diversity of people. This curiosity makes the junior years a prime time for stimulating interest in missions, both local and worldwide. Rather than merely informing students about missionaries and their work, periodically provide a missions-related project which allows juniors to get directly involved in some aspect of missions. Below are several specific projects your group can undertake for a focus on world missions.

ADOPT A MISSIONARY

These projects require preparation, so begin your planning at least a month or two in advance. Focus on the specific ministries your church supports.

Get addresses of missionaries to whom students can write. Choose missionaries who do various types of missionary service (teaching children, training pastors, medical services, literature distribution, etc.). You may want to focus on one part of the world or explore missions work in several different countries. Juniors will especially enjoy corresponding with missionaries who have children close to their own age.

Write to these missionaries. Say, for example, "In four or five weeks students in our Sunday School will be studying missions. In order to make our study more meaningful we would appreciate your letting us know: (1) Information about the country in which you live. (2) Your job. (3) Specific things we can pray about. (4) A project or small gift of money we can share with you." Ask the missionary what is the best way to reimburse him or her for expenses in responding to your request.

Research the needs of missionaries for which your juniors can pray. Pool information from staff and church members who are in contact with missionaries. List specific needs a missionary may have—money, supplies, friends, schools for children. Does he or she need prayer for learning a new language? prayer for more believers? prayer that believers grow in their faith? With a little research, children can begin to pray specifically, and to thank God for specific answers!

Plan a project to involve the students in giving their time, money or possessions to help a missionary. Contact your church missions committee or denominational office for information. Or the idea for your project may come directly from your correspondence with the missionaries. For example, you may choose to:

- make puppets for children's ministry;
- collect food, clothing, toys, books;
- cut out and organize Bible story pictures;
- write letters to children in the community where the missionary lives;
- send birthday cards to missionary family members;
- record cassette tapes of students telling Bible stories or singing;
- raise money for a specific need.

Your students will be pleased to have a special role.

Make a poster or tabletop display for your project. Let the students suggest something they can do without (such as ice cream, candy, toys, part of their allowance) in order to be able to give to the project. Suggest several household chores students may offer to do for money to contribute. Use a glass jar to collect the visible results, or create a chart which shows progress towards your goal.

OTHER PROJECT IDEAS

You may also wish to choose from the following ideas to enhance students' understanding and involvement in missions.

1. Schedule a **visitor** to tell or read a true mission story. Your guest may be a missionary or one who has visited missionaries at work. Juniors respond well to high school or college students who have been on short-term mission assignments. Before the guest arrives, have the class write questions to ask the guest. Later they can make a report as a group about what they have learned.

2. Begin a **cassette tape exchange.** Make a cassette tape to mail to your missionaries. Include songs and Bible verses from the group, news about your Sunday School activities, and questions the students want to ask.

(Continued on next page.)

(Continued from previous page.)

Let the students do the asking. "Hello! My name is Adam. I would like to know if . . . ?" The missionary will be able to answer Adam (and the group) specifically.

Also record the students praying for missions. The prayers of the students will encourage the missionaries.

Enclose a blank tape for missionaries to reply with songs, news and answers to questions. Also enclose a self-addressed, stamped cassette mailer for return of the tape.

3. Make a **display** for others in your church to see what your class has learned about missions. To make the display interesting and attractive, send the missionaries an international money order to purchase film for snapshots or for curios they can send which you can display. (Or items may be purchased from an imported goods store.) Have the class plan the display. The ideas behind the display will remain with them longer if they have had a part in the planning.

4. Make a chart listing the **birthdays of missionaries and their children.** Make cards for upcoming birthdays and/or holidays.

5. Listen to a **recording in the lan-guage of a missionary's country and learn a song** in that language.

6. Have a **picture exchange.** Duplicate missionary pictures so each class member can have one as a prayer reminder. Send pictures of your class to the missionaries so they can also have prayer reminders for you.

7. **View a missions film or video.**

8. **Set up a missions book corner in your classroom.** Purchase or borrow books about the lives of famous missionaries. Encourage students to check out the books to read during the week.

MOTIVATE YOUR STUDENTS TO LEARN

There is a direct relationship between a student's motivation to learn and the effectiveness of the learning process. How can we motivate fifth and sixth graders to want to learn?

Consider the following suggestions for motivating juniors. Although not every idea will be effective with every student, never give up! As long as communication between teacher and student exists, there is an opportunity for increasing a child's desire to participate and to learn.

1. **Know your students.** This concept can never be overemphasized. Become well acquainted with each student in your class. Know individual interests, abilities and skills. Your insights will enable you to increase motivation for participation and learning as you help the student to recognize abilities, use skills and respond to areas of personal interest. Very often, a seemingly unmotivated student will gladly participate in activities that capitalize on his or her interests and abilities.

2. **Plan for juniors to have a choice of activities.** When a student is allowed to choose between equally acceptable options, the act of choosing is in itself a way of increasing interest. Allowing choices of ways to complete an activity (e.g., deciding on use of chalk, paint or crayons for a mural) also increases interest and motivation.

3. **Provide opportunities for juniors to interact and cooperate with each other.** Most juniors respond favorably to working together in small groups, in pairs or in the total group. As juniors get to know each other better, motivation increases. When juniors are asked to complete a task in a small group, each student may be given a specific responsibility to help the group work together (one student gets needed supplies, one student records the groups' work, one student acts as timekeeper, etc.).

4. **Listen attentively.** An adult who listens to what a student has to say provides immediate incentive for that student to cooperate and participate in learning experiences.

5. **Be flexible in your teaching procedure.** Too much predictability leads to boredom for both juniors and teachers. Although a program needs stability, a good program is balanced by change and flexibility. Plan enough variety in the kinds of activities you provide—especially at the beginning of the session—so that students are curious to find out what they will be doing at each session.

6. **Provide opportunities for juniors to help other people.** For example, a service project catches the imagination and enthusiasm of fifth and sixth graders as a firsthand way to put God's Word into action.

LEARNING CHECKLIST

☐ **How does each student feel about being in your class?**

☐ **Do both you and the students look forward to studying God's Word together?**

☐ **Does each student have your acceptance and support?**

☐ **Is there an atmosphere of warmth and happiness?**

☐ **Is there an opportunity for each student to succeed?**

☐ **Are choices provided?**

☐ **How do you insure a relaxed pace, free from time pressure?**

☐ **How are you helping juniors build relationships with one another?**

☐ **Are your expectations of juniors realistic and consistent?**

TEACHING JUNIORS TO PRAY

One of the most challenging tasks facing a teacher of juniors is how to build a climate where students will be comfortable praying in the group. In order for juniors to make prayer a meaningful part of their daily lives, they need group prayer experiences to provide positive patterns they can imitate.

PATTERNS FOR IMITATION

1. **Keep your own prayers simple, brief and personal.** Your students need to see you pray. Just as Jesus' example motivated his disciples to want to learn to pray (Luke 11:1), you are a model of prayer for the students you teach. They need to hear prayers that they can duplicate. They also need to hear prayers that really matter to you, not mere formalities or vague declarations. Thus, you must become transparent to your class, sharing some of your doubts, struggles and anxieties.

2. **Focus prayer time on issues of concern to the class.** If you want students to care about prayer, then pray for what they already care about. Listen to their conversations to gain insight into issues and events which concern and interest them. Ask them to tell what they enjoy or what causes them worry. Demonstrate an attitude of interest and caring as you talk with juniors about the items they share. Then pray with them about those concerns.

(**NOTE:** Some of the most meaningful prayer times occur one-on-one when a student mentions something in informal conversation and a teacher offers to pray about it on the spot.)

3. **Structure prayer as conversation with God.** Avoid making prayer a recitation of problems for God to solve. Establish a model of talking with God about the good and the bad, the fun and the serious, the joys and sorrows of life. Avoid archaic language and Christian jargon. Juniors need to experience communication with God that is both respectful and highly personal.

4. **Invite students to suggest items to pray about.** Once you have established a pattern of openly talking about and informally praying for things of importance to your students, then, encouraging students to suggest prayer requests becomes very meaningful. Without the foundation of supportive, personal sharing, asking students to mention things to pray about has a tendency to elicit a litany of "safe" requests (Grandma's bad knee, dead goldfish, etc.) or announcements about upcoming events ("Pray for my birthday party on Tuesday afternoon."). Elicit prayer requests about the lesson topic by asking questions such as "When is a time you need God's help in saying only good things about others?"

5. **Invite volunteers to each pray for one item.** Students who are comfortable in mentioning things to pray about are not threatened by praying aloud for one of those items. Especially if a pattern of simple, brief prayers has already been set.

GUIDELINES FOR BUILDING KIDS' PRAYER LIVES

1. **Make prayer an important time in your class session.** If classroom prayer is haphazard, boring, or an "add-on" after everything else is done, juniors will not be drawn to want to pray on their own.

2. **Share incidents from your own prayer experiences.** Talk with your class about your own prayer times during the week. When do you pray? What did you pray about this week? What benefits do you feel you gained from your prayer times?

3. **Ask, "What can I pray about for you this next week?"** When you talk informally with juniors, before, during, or after class, make a point of finding out what is happening in their lives. Then let them know you'll make a point of praying about that in the next few days.

4. **Ask, "What have you been praying about this past week?"** Once your students are familiar with prayer in your classroom and your example

(Continued on next page.)

(Continued from previous page.)

of personal prayer, encourage them to pray on their own. One way to do this is to suggest that each student choose to pray during the week for one concern raised by class members. Then make a point to ask students about their previous weeks' prayer experiences.

5. **Encourage prayer journals.** Juniors can gain a great deal of satisfaction from a written record of their prayer times. Provide small notebooks for each student to use in writing a few sentences after each prayer. The journal may contain prayer requests and answers, but should focus on the student's thoughts and feelings about prayer.

IDEAS FOR WAYS TO VARY PRAYER TIME

1. **Silent prayer.** Suggest one thing for everyone to pray about silently, then allow 15 to 20 seconds of silence. Encourage students to talk about this prayer experience. Many people find it difficult to focus their attention when all is quiet. One approach students may try is to imagine themselves bowing before God as He asks, "What do you want to say to me right now?"

2. **Completion prayers.** One at a time, suggest a variety of prayer sentences students can complete: "I praise You, God, because...," "You have been good to me by...," "One problem I need Your help with is...," "Please help me not to be worried about...," etc. Complete each sentence yourself, then invite volunteers to offer their own completions.

3. **Conversational prayer.** Invite students to talk to God as they would to a close friend. Suggest these three rules:

   • Pray about just one thing, then give someone else a turn.

   • Before you pray about something else, tell God what you think about what the previous person just said.

   • Talk to God about what's going on in your life. Don't just keep asking for things.

4. **Build a prayer.** Either on hand-out sheets or lettered on the chalkboard

or a poster, provide a variety of different prayer statements from which students can choose. Include two or more options for each part of a prayer: the address, praise for who God is, thanks for what He has done, prayer for others, personal requests, closing. For example, options for the address could be: "Dear God," "Dear Heavenly Father," "Wonderful Lord," etc.

5. **Written prayers.** Putting thoughts and feelings in writing is often less threatening than speaking them aloud. After prayers have been written, invite volunteers to read at least part of what they wrote. Respect the right of confidentiality in these prayers.

6. **Pray-as-you-go.** Rather than compiling a list of requests and praises and then praying about them, invite a volunteer to pray for each item as it is mentioned.

7. **Topical prayers.** Focus prayers on a particular theme or topic, preferably related to the day's lesson or to a current issue of major interest to students. For example, when studying about serving others, lead the class in prayers of thanks for those who have served them, in prayers for development of willing attitudes to serve, and in prayers for awareness of opportunities to be of service.

BUILDING RELATIONSHIPS WITH JUNIORS

Some teachers just conduct classes. They tell Bible stories and lead activities. They prepare materials, mark attendance and keep order. Other teachers do these same things, but with an important difference. They also change lives. The students who are in their classes are never the same afterwards. What makes the difference?

Some teachers appear to attract juniors like the proverbial Pied Piper. These teachers seem to be gifted with a natural talent which others merely envy, convinced they cannot attain similar results. Fortunately, there are a few basic skills that can be learned easily and used effectively to build positive relationships with juniors.

Teachers who practice these skills find their teaching becomes more enjoyable, and students respond openly to teachers who care enough to work at improving relationships. The skills which help build relationships with juniors include both nonverbal and verbal skills.

NONVERBAL SKILLS

1. **Expression**—Welcome each student with a friendly smile and a warm greeting—and don't let it be the last smile of the session!

2. **Position**—Sit at the students' level. Avoid hovering over juniors or moving mysteriously behind them.

Join in the lesson activities whenever you can, instead of merely supervising what students are doing. For example, play a game, act out a skit or share a prayer request along with kids.

3. **Listen**—Children are drawn to the teacher who listens. Most adults tend to nod absentmindedly, thinking ahead to what THEY are going to say next. Instead, focus attention on the student who is talking, listening with your eyes, your face, your hands and your body.

4. **Touch**—A pat on the hand or shoulder says, "I like you, you are worthwhile." Be sensitive to the unique needs of each youngster, respecting the personal space of a student while making it clear you are there to be a friend.

5. **Gesture**—Nod your head in response as a student talks with you. Lean forward to show interest. Gesture with an open hand instead of a pointing finger or closed fist. Include each student in the group with a broad sweep of the arms, or indicate specific students with a wave or nod.

6. **Provide materials**—Build juniors' confidence by the simple act of providing interesting materials for students to use. Taking the time to secure props for a skit, colorful paper for an art activity, an occasional treat, etc., are indicators of a concern which kids appreciate.

VERBAL SKILLS

1. **Accept feelings**—Accepting means listening deeply, sensing and feeling the student's real emotions, and responding with honest empathy, even if not always with agreement. Say, "Darren says he sometimes hits his brother when his brother bugs him. Darren, you must really feel angry when your brother teases you." Later, in your class discussion you can refer again to this situation asking, "What is something better you could do when your brother or sister bugs you? What advice does our Bible passage give for a situation like that?"

2. **Accept ideas**—Accepting ideas helps students dare to think out loud. It provides freedom to ask questions or express ideas, enabling students to expand their concepts without fear of being put down if they give a "wrong" answer.

Many adults tend to pass over what a student actually said (or tried to say), jumping in with "better" comments as soon as the youngster is finished. Adults often want to improve on or correct a student's contributions, giving the "right" answer instead.

While "right" answers are important, it is more important to help the student be ready to discover or receive that answer. If a junior feels

(Continued on next page.)

(Continued from previous page.)

the teacher has belittled his or her efforts, there is little interest in the "right" answers. Focus on using what the student says or does, letting the student know that his or her thoughts, emotions and actions have value.

3. **Praise and encourage**—All kids (as well as adults) need to feel good about themselves and what they are accomplishing. Most adults are much quicker to criticize than they are to praise. Instead, make a point of looking for reasons to commend students (and be willing to overlook some of their imperfections). At the same time, be aware that juniors tend to be embarrassed if an adult "makes a fuss" over something.

Effective encouragement and praise must be:

◆ specific, telling the student exactly what was done well;

◆ honest, not offering inflated evaluation;

◆ appropriate, fitting the task of the specific student, and also the common desire of juniors not to be "fussed" over;

◆ frequent, especially in the early stages of new learning.

4. **Ask open questions**—Most teachers ask questions. However, questions that require one correct answer are threatening to many juniors. Instead, remove pressure by asking students for their opinions, feelings or ideas, not just to repeat facts they have heard or read.

A few stimulating questions include:

◆ What was the person trying to do?

◆ Why do you think the Bible tells us to do this?

◆ Which do you think is better...?

◆ Which part of the (story, verse, song) reminded you of something you've experienced?

◆ How do you think the person felt when...?

◆ What might have happened if...?

◆ Why was this an important experience for...?

◆ When has something like this happened to you?

These verbal and nonverbal skills are helpful for every teacher. Their use will more effectively communicate Bible truths and content while building positive shared experiences between teacher and students. Initially, some of these techniques may seem awkward. However, with practice they become natural and effective ways of building positive relationships with juniors—relationships that will carry over beyond the classroom.

AN IMPORTANT NOTE:

One very practical aspect of building relationships with juniors involves the ratio of teachers to students in your group. The larger the ratio, the more difficult it is to build relationships. In most once-a-week programs staffed by volunteers, it has proven wise to strive to maintain a ratio of *one teacher for up to eight juniors.*

While there may be highly skilled and motivated teachers who can succeed with larger groups, it is unwise to expect most volunteers to work under circumstances which require exceptional effort in order to succeed. At times it may be necessary to work with larger ratios, but teachers and leaders should make it a matter of prayer and serious discussion to find ways to involve additional people in this ministry.

CHECKLIST FOR MEETING STUDENTS' NEEDS

Use this checklist as a tool to evaluate the ways you meet the needs of the students in your class. Check the box which most correctly answers each of the questions below.

		Always	Often	Some-times	Seldom	Never
PHYSICAL	**DO YOU...**					
	◆ provide adequate lighting for reading?					
	◆ keep the room temperature and air circulation comfortable?					
	◆ provide enough space and arrange furnishings in a way for students to participate in active learning?					
	◆ plan a variety of styles of learning activities during the quarter?					
SOCIAL	**DO YOU...**					
	◆ show sensitivity to your students' problems and feelings?					
	◆ share personal feelings and experiences from your Christian life?					
	◆ encourage your students to work together?					
	◆ provide the security of a few rules that are consistently enforced?					
EMOTIONAL/MENTAL	**DO YOU...**					
	◆ avoid using "put-downs" when opinions or ideas are different from yours?					
	◆ see your class as individuals rather than as a group?					
	◆ listen to your students?					
	◆ affirm your students for sharing and cooperating in class?					
	◆ provide creative ways for students to express ideas and use abilities and interests?					
	◆ plan ways to involve each student?					
	◆ have an awareness of the vocabulary level of your students?					
SPIRITUAL	**DO YOU...**					
	◆ help your students use the Bible to discover Bible truths for themselves?					
	◆ help your students identify with Bible characters as real people?					
	◆ actively seek to discover each student's spiritual condition and attitudes?					
	◆ express enthusiasm about being a Christian?					

GET ACQUAINTED!

Name of student: _____

1. Briefly describe this student's family.
   ◆ Parent(s) Names: Notable Information

   _____   _____

   _____   _____

   _____   _____

   _____   _____

   ◆ Brothers/Sisters (place in order of birth):

   _____   _____

   _____   _____

   ◆ Other information you know about the student's home situation that will help you teach and relate to the student.

2. What school subject does this student like most? Least?

3. What is the student's favorite activity?

4. How would you describe this student's spiritual growth?

5. Name two of this student's closest friends from church.

6. How does the student feel about coming to your class or program?

7. What character quality concerns this student's parents most at this time?

8. What lesson or activity has interested the student most in recent weeks?

WHAT ABOUT ME?

NAME: _____

(But some people call me _____

HERE'S WHO i LIVE WITH:

AT SCHOOL THE CLASS i LIKE THE MOST IS...

AND THE CLASS i LIKE THE LEAST iS...

AFTER SCHOOL OR ON WEEKENDS MY FAVORITE THING TO DO IS...

LEADING YOUR PRETEEN STUDENTS TO CHRIST

Many adult Christians look back to their upper-elementary years as the time when they accepted Christ as Savior. Not only are juniors able to understand the difference between right and wrong and their own personal need of forgiveness, they are also interested in Jesus' death and resurrection as the means by which God provides salvation. In addition, students at this age are capable of growing in their faith through prayer, Bible reading, worship and service.

However, juniors are still limited in their understanding, and immature in following through on their intentions and commitments. As such, they need thoughtful, patient guidance in coming to know Christ personally and continuing to grow in Him.

1. PRAY

Ask God to prepare the students in your class to receive the good news about Jesus and prepare you to effectively communicate with them.

2. PRESENT THE GOOD NEWS.

Use words and phrases that students understand. Avoid symbolism that will confuse these literal-minded thinkers. *Discuss these points slowly enough to allow time for thinking and comprehending.*

a. God wants you to become His child. Do you know why God wants you in His family? (see 1 John 4:8).

b. You and all the people in the world have done wrong things. The Bible word for doing wrong is *sin*. What do you think should happen to us when we sin? (see Romans 6:23).

c. God loves you so much, He sent His Son to die on the cross for your sin. Because Jesus never sinned, He is the only one who can take the punishment for your sin (see 1 Corinthians 15:3; 1 John 4:14).

d. Are you sorry for your sin? Tell God that you are. Do you believe Jesus died to take the punishment for your sin? If you tell God you are sorry for your sin and tell Him you do believe and accept Jesus' death to take away your sin— God forgives all your sin (see John 1:12).

e. The Bible says that when you believe in Jesus, God's Son, you receive God's gift of eternal life. This gift makes you a child of God. This means God is with you now and forever (see John 3:16).

As you give students many opportunities to think about what it means to be a Christian, expose them to a variety of lessons and descriptions of the meaning of salvation to aid their understanding.

3. TALK INDIVIDUALLY WITH STUDENTS.

Talking about salvation one-on-one creates opportunities to ask and answer questions. Ask questions that move the student beyond simple yes-or-no answers or recitation of memorized information. Ask open-ended, "what do you think?" questions such as:

- Why do you think it's important to...?
- What are some things you really like about Jesus?
- Why do you think that Jesus died because of wrong things you and I have done?
- What difference do you think it makes for a person to be forgiven?

Answers to these open-ended questions will help you discern how much the student does or does not understand.

4. OFFER OPPORTUNITIES WITHOUT PRESSURE.

Fifth and sixth graders are still children, vulnerable to being manipulated by adults. A good way to guard against coercing a student's response is to simply pause periodically and ask, "Would you like to hear more about this now or at another time?" Loving acceptance of the student, even when he or she is not fully inter-

(Continued on next page.)

(Continued from previous page.)

ested in pursuing the matter, is crucial in building and maintaining positive attitudes toward becoming part of God's family.

5. GIVE TIME TO THINK AND PRAY.

There is great value in encouraging a student to think and pray about what you have said before making a response. Also allow moments for quiet thinking about questions you ask.

6. RESPECT THE STUDENT'S RESPONSE.

Whether or not a student declares faith in Jesus Christ, there is a need for adults to accept the student's action. There is also a need to realize that a student's initial responses to Jesus are just the beginning of a life-long process of growing in the faith.

7. GUIDE THE STUDENT IN FURTHER GROWTH.

Here are three important parts in the nurturing process:

a. *Talk regularly about your relationship with God.* As you talk about your relationship, the stu-

dent will begin to feel that it's OK to talk about such things. Then you can comfortably ask the student to share his or her thoughts and feelings, and encourage the student to ask questions of you.

b. *Prepare the student to deal with doubts.* Emphasize that certainty about salvation is not dependent on our feelings or doing enough good deeds. Show the student places in God's Word that clearly declare that salvation comes by grace through faith (i.e., John 1:12; Ephesians 2:8,9; Hebrews 11:6; 1 John 5:11).

c. *Teach the student to confess all sin.* To confess means to admit or to agree. Confessing sins means agreeing with God that we really have sinned. Assure the student that confession always results in forgiveness.

A NON-TYPICAL SESSION

There is probably no class of fifth and/or sixth graders that can be considered truly typical. Every class is as unique as each of the young people in the class. Every teacher is different, too! Some teachers like to use active learning games, some prefer guiding discussions, and some prefer helping their classes work on projects. With all these differences, no curriculum can guarantee that every activity it suggests will work with every class or for every teacher.

Whatever teaching style you prefer, try to be as flexible as possible in planning each session. To accommodate your class's unique blend of unique individuals, each session should combine activity and schedule choices. Be willing to try something new, and to vary the way you usually do things. Give yourself the opportunity to meet students' needs for involvement, as well as building the relationships with your students that make the difference between simply conducting a class and leading students to follow your example in knowing and loving Jesus Christ.

The following major segments of a balanced session plan provide a flexible pattern you can easily adapt to meet the needs of your students.

DISCOVER   5-15 MINUTES

Begin your session with one or more activities which help build relationships among students and capture interest in the topic of the day. If there is any part of a session where you should risk being out of the ordinary, it is these opening activities. Variety at the beginning will pay rich dividends throughout the session by stimulating interest and anticipation.

◆ If you teach alone, offer one activity. If you teach with someone else, each of you may lead a different activity, offering students a choice.

◆ Make sure at least one of the activities can easily accommodate students who arrive at various times. Think of how an activity can engage the interest of the first one or two students who arrive, and then gradually add others as they come into the room.

◆ Vary the physical arrangement of the room. If last week you began the session around tables, this week have students work on the chalkboard or sheets of paper mounted on the wall. Or gather on the floor. It only takes a few moments of moving chairs to create a sense that something different is happening this week.

◆ Think of ways to involve that student who arrives early. Take time to talk about events of the week. Provide an activity from your Student Guide which can be done before class. Often several students enjoy practicing a script to be presented later in the session. With a little planning ahead each week, your students will look forward eagerly to the start of another interesting session.

STUDY   20-30 MINUTES

Every session needs a segment in which you guide students to read, study and discuss the Bible for themselves.

◆ To accomplish that goal, make sure each student or pair of students has a Bible. If students do not bring Bibles from home, provide classroom Bibles and bookmarks (slips of paper, student-decorated index cards, etc.) to aid in locating passages to be studied.

◆ Ask questions which encourage students to observe and interpret what the Bible says. Guide students to discover what the Bible says and what it means. This will help both students who feel they already

(Continued on next page.)

(Continued from previous page.)

"know" all the Bible stories and those to whom the Bible is totally unfamiliar.

◆ Rather than being the one to tell the class what the Bible says, guide them in developing good Bible-study skills, learning to use the Bible themselves.

◆ Vary your approach to Bible study. Your students will enjoy a humorous script or other interactive idea. Provide opportunities to explore Bible narratives, character studies, inspirational passages, short verses.

◆ Use music to give your study a contemporary flavor. Have them listen to and/or sing Scripture set to melody. Words that are sung will be remembered longer than words which are spoken.

◆ Before you finish your preparation, write a one-sentence summary of the key point you want students to grasp. Then make sure your teaching approaches will focus students' understanding on that lesson's Bible truth.

APPLY   20-30 MINUTES

Every session needs time focused on helping students explore the relationship between the Bible truth they have been studying and their day-to-day experiences. If you teach with one or more teachers, each of you may lead an activity as a way to give students variety and choice. Over a period of weeks, seek to provide a balance of different types of learning activities.

◆ Always prepare about a half dozen thought-provoking questions to guide the students to think and respond as they complete the learning activity.

◆ Sometimes plan a discussion option that engages students in thoughtful dialog. To stimulate discussion, use idea starters such as current events articles and guest interviews from your church family.

◆ At other times, provide an active option, such as a game or other activity that incorporates physical movement.

◆ Include periodic service projects, as well as music, art, skits, cooking, and more!

◆ Prayer provides a natural conclusion to this segment. As with all other session components, vary your approach to prayer. For example, at times lead a prayer of thanksgiving or praise; at other times pray for a specific need of concern to the entire class. Many teachers find it works well to plan a longer time once a unit for students to talk about prayer requests and pray together.

A REMINDER ABOUT RATIOS AND ROOMS

Meaningful discussion of life application will be most effective if you maintain a **ratio** of one teacher for up to six to eight students, with no more than 30 students in a classroom. If you are short-handed, recruit parent-helpers to assist, participating in their child's class for a unit (four or five lessons) at a time.

Energetic juniors learn best in a **room** with adequate space for active participation: 25 to 30 square feet for each student. When kids are crowded, behavior problems increase and learning effectiveness decreases.

WHY ARE YOU TEACHING PRETEENS?

Anyone who approaches a group of preteens is likely to have butterflies in the stomach, sweaty palms, and/or a catch in the throat. Such nervousness, while common, is not usually a fear that the kids may get out of hand. The real source of apprehension is a sense that teaching juniors about God is a vitally important ministry that will challenge the very best anyone has to offer. There are three important questions every teacher of juniors needs to thoughtfully—and prayerfully—consider.

1. WHY SHOULD I TEACH PRETEENS?

There are many reasons people give for how they first got involved teaching juniors:

"Someone begged me to do it."
"I had a child in the group and felt I should help out."
"No one else was willing to do it."
"I felt guilty."
"I really like kids this age."
"The adult classes were boring."
"I needed a responsibility to push me to get up on Sunday mornings."

While the above reasons are commonly given, none of them have the power to make teaching a deeply satisfying experience. Consider the following three reasons for making time in your busy life to share God's love and His Word with juniors:

◆ Every child is worth teaching because every child is filled with God-given potential. What can compare with helping to influence a child to discover God's wonderful purpose for living?

◆ Jesus clearly showed the high value of a child. He placed a child in the middle of His disciples and said, "Whoever welcomes a little child like this in my name welcomes me" (Matthew 18:5).

◆ Teaching juniors helps you reach your own potential. Just being around juniors is valuable for grown-ups who are open to learning from the openness, enthusiasm, and curiosity of children. Add to that the challenge of trying to communicate God's Word in meaningful ways for juniors and you have a guaranteed formula for nudging adults out of their comfort zones—a prerequisite to personal and spiritual growth.

2. IF I WEREN'T TEACHING JUNIORS, WHAT WOULD I BE DOING INSTEAD?

While there are bound to be mornings when a Sunday School teacher mutters, "I'd rather stay in bed," the choice is not really between doing something and doing nothing. The time involved in teaching would be used for something else. Another way to ask this question is, "If I weren't teaching juniors, would I be doing something of greater or lesser value instead?" Or, "Is there anything else I could do with my time that could be more worthwhile?"

3. HOW WILL I KNOW IF MY TEACHING MAKES A DIFFERENCE?

No one wants to invest time and energy in "going through the motions," "filling in," or "holding class." Expressions such as these all convey a sense of dutiful, but unfulfilling labor. There can be no spark of excitement and challenge without a clear expectation of accomplishment. To avoid merely "holding class," focus on these four powerful factors which make a ministry to preteens truly effective:

◆ **Build Relationships**—Juniors are influenced through relationships more than through any other aspect of teaching. In order to build positive relationships with the juniors you teach, make the effort to get to know and care about each one personally. A good start is to pray for a different child every day.

◆ **Meet Needs**—There is little satisfaction in teaching lessons; there is great satisfaction in discovering the real needs (physical, emotional, social and spiritual) of students and then prayerfully working to develop skills in meeting those needs.

◆ **Have Fun**—While the goal of teaching is not to have fun, a healthy dose of enjoyment contributes greatly to teaching success. If you enjoy the class, the students will be likely to enjoy it, and to learn and grow from it.

◆ **Watch for Growth**—Neither you nor your students are perfect. Rather than viewing the imperfections in students as annoyances which get in the way of learning, see them as opportunities for growth to occur. Your patient, loving guidance can influence positive changes that will last a lifetime!

JUNIORS IN ADULT WORSHIP

Are the preteens in your church expected to attend your church service? What do your fifth and sixth graders gain from being in the adult worship service? What steps can you take to help your fifth and sixth graders understand and participate meaningfully in your church's worship experiences?

Churches differ widely in their approach to including children in worship:

◆ Some provide separate children's programming for everyone under Junior High age, and actively discourage any youngsters "sneaking" into church.

◆ Some consider their worship service a time for the whole family to be together and welcome (or at least tolerate) infants, toddlers, preschoolers and everyone else.

◆ Some provide child care or instructional children's programs for the younger ages, and pick some point in the childhood years as the time to group children with everyone else.

◆ Some expect some or all children to attend the first part of the adult worship service, then those below a designated age or grade level are dismissed to a children's program.

◆ Some include some feature intended specifically for children in their worship service (children's sermon, hymn or chorus, bulletin, etc.).

No matter what choice a church makes, there will be some problems, whether juniors are already used to attending the worship service or are just being introduced to it. These problems reflect the big differences between children, even fifth and sixth graders, and adults: differences in ability to sit still, differences in attention span, vocabulary, interests and needs.

In most cases, the resulting problems are dealt with by the children themselves, but the outcome is often not what adults intended. Juniors are adept at developing a host of devices to keep themselves occupied when surrounded by adults: daydreaming, counting ceiling tiles, pestering parents, squirming, rummaging in pockets and purses, etc. Once a child has learned to tune out his or her surroundings, it becomes increasingly difficult to capture that child's attention and gain meaningful participation.

While the differences between kids and adults cannot be erased until the children become adults themselves, there are specific steps you can take to help minimize problems when the students you teach mingle with grown-ups in worship.

1. Identify the Purpose for Having Juniors Attend Worship.

While churches differ in their approach to involving children in worship, children's leaders tend to identify very similar objectives for the children who attend the worship service. Check any of these commonly mentioned goals which your church has for the children who attend your worship service:

❑ Help children feel a sense of belonging to the church family, getting to know the church leaders and people.

❑ Bring family members together instead of separating them.

❑ Allow children to learn how our church worships by observing parents and other adults.

❑ Let children enjoy participating in worship experiences (music, prayer, etc.).

❑ Provide children with an additional opportunity for learning about God.

Unfortunately, sitting a student in a pew does not guarantee that those intended purposes will automatically be accomplished.

2. Evaluate Your Worship Service from a Junior's Perspective.

Next, look at the various parts of your worship service in light of your goals for having juniors present. Observe your juniors during these common worship service activities. Ask them what they find interesting or boring about each segment:

◆ Welcome when arriving
◆ Group singing
◆ Announcements
◆ Scripture reading
◆ Children's feature
◆ Prayer requests/praises
◆ Prayer time
◆ Offering
◆ Greeting others nearby
◆ Special observances (baptism, communion, etc.)
◆ Special music
◆ Sermon

Often, what juniors really experience at these times is significantly different from the experience of adults. For example, most churches try to help people feel welcome and comfortable in the church service. Friendly people are enlisted to smile and shake hands and offer a friendly word as people arrive. Many churches also include time for people to stand and greet

(Continued on next page.)

(Continued from previous page.)

those around them. However, these friendship rituals tend to leave children either ignored or uncomfortable.

◆ Adults tend to talk to each other, ignoring the children.

◆ Many children do not even bother to stand up when everyone else begins shaking hands, indicating they do not feel part of the interaction taking place.

3. Prepare Your Juniors for Their Worship Service Experiences.

The following ideas are not guaranteed to make all juniors enjoy and benefit from all aspects of adult church services. But they can help your students gain more of the intended benefits of being in the worship service. Every week, during your class session, insert a reference to the worship service your juniors may attend (or may have already attended). For example:

◆ Tell your class one reason you like to attend the worship service. (Be willing to admit if you do not fully enjoy every part of every service. Kids need to know they are not the only ones who sometimes may be bored.)

◆ Remind students to visit the restroom and drinking fountain before entering the service.

◆ Encourage students to arrive for worship a few minutes before the service begins and do the following things to get ready:

1. Say hello to at least one usher or greeter. (For several weeks in a row, or once in awhile, arrange with a different usher/greeter each week to have a small candy or other treat to give to any junior who shakes his or her hand.)

2. Wave, smile, or say hello to someone else you already know.

3. Sit near the front so you feel you're a part of what's going on.

4. Find at least one thing in the bulletin that is going to happen during the service. For example, locate the page of the first hymn to be sung, or look up the Scripture to be read.

5. Whisper a short prayer before the service starts.

◆ Encourage juniors to look and listen for something in the service to ask you a question about afterwards.

◆ Tell something you learned or were reminded of during the service that you feel is important for your life.

◆ Affirm specific children for ways you observed them participating and showing positive behavior.

◆ Discuss what to do when you realize you have stopped paying attention. For example:

• Silently pray, telling God you're having a hard time listening.

• Look at the bulletin to remind yourself about what is going on.

• Take a few deep breaths (quietly), then listen to find out what is being said that is important.

• Draw a picture of what is being talked about.

4. Involve Students in Making Worship Services More "Kid-Friendly."

Most church leaders would like to make the worship service more meaningful and enjoyable for children. They just need an occasional nudge and a few workable ideas in order to do so. Juniors are old enough to accept the responsibility and privilege of trying to improve things in the life of the church. Here are a few ideas they will enjoy:

◆ Write letters to the church's worship leaders, thanking them for

their leadership roles in the worship service.

◆ Periodically invite worship service leaders (pastor, music director, usher, choir member, etc.) to visit your class and talk about what he or she does in the worship service. This will help those leaders to recognize the presence of children as part of the congregation.

◆ Brainstorm a list of ways to make the worship service more interesting and beneficial for kids. A few ideas they might consider putting on their list:

• Ushers and greeters remember to welcome children.

• Sing at least one hymn or song which can easily be learned and sung by children.

• Mention children, not just adults during prayer time or in the sermon.

• Provide a children's bulletin or worksheet to each child.

• Find ways to actively involve juniors. Give kids a chance to:
✓ read the Scripture passage or a special announcement,
✓ hand out bulletins,
✓ assist the greeters in welcoming people,
✓ collect the offering,
✓ hold up a sign or poster to help with an announcement or to emphasize a point in the sermon,
✓ participate in special music,
✓ interview the pastor or other leader,
✓ place transparencies on the overhead projector,
✓ move a microphone or prop when needed.

Let the group select the best ideas suggested, copy them into a letter or report, and submit it to the church's worship leaders for their consideration.

GAMES

Never again will you be at a loss for games
to play with fifth and sixth graders!
Here are dozens of great games
to supplement every part of your Bible lesson,
as well as party games and mixers.

INCLUDED ARE:

☛ Bible Memory Games
☛ Bible Story Review Games
☛ Life Application Games
☛ Just-for-Fun Games

WRITTEN IN STONE

Materials Checklist

◆ Bible
◆ large piece of cardboard
◆ gray paint
◆ paintbrush
◆ black felt pen
◆ utility knife

Optional—

◆ use gray poster board

Preparation: Paint the cardboard gray on both sides. After cardboard dries, cut out two large tablet shapes. Letter the Bible Memory Passage on each tablet. Cut each tablet into 10 pieces (see sketch). The two sets should be identical.

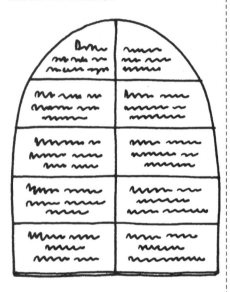

Procedure: Lay all 20 tablet pieces facedown in random order. Students take turns turning over two tablet pieces at a time. When non-matching pieces are turned over, they are turned facedown again in their original places. When matching pieces are turned over, player puts them both faceup where the group can see them. When all tablet pieces have been matched, students put them together in correct order to make two complete tablets. Students read passage aloud.

MUSICAL PRAISE

Materials Checklist

◆ Bible
◆ music cassette
◆ one chair for each student
◆ masking tape
◆ bright piece of paper or fabric
◆ cassette player
◆ butcher paper and felt pen or chalkboard and chalk
◆ 8-12 index cards

Preparation: Letter the Bible Memory Passage on chalkboard or paper and display in visible location. Place chairs in a large circle, facing inward. Tape a bright piece of paper or fabric to one chair.

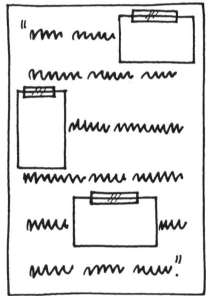

Procedure: As you play music, students walk around circle of chairs. When music stops, each student sits in a chair. The student sitting in the marked chair stands up and tapes an index card over any part of the passage, horizontally or vertically (see sketch). The class then recites the passage. Continue playing game until all words are covered and students are able to say the entire passage from memory. (For longer passages, do one verse at a time.)

SKIPPIN' STREET SMARTS

Materials Checklist

◆ Bible
◆ chalkboard and chalk or poster board and felt pen
◆ a long jump rope

Preparation: On chalkboard or poster board, letter Bible Memory Passage, underlining syllables or words to produce an interesting rhythm pattern, as shown in sketch. (Each number equals one beat.)

Every-	one	should	be
1	2	3	4
quick to	listen,	slow to	speak,
5	6	7	8
and slow to	become	an-	gry.
9	10	11	12

Procedure: Using rhythm pattern you created, read passage aloud with students. Repeat several times.

Choose two assistants or students to twirl the jump rope. Jumpers line up behind a designated starting point. First player tries to jump in and over the rope as the rope is twirled slowly. Once the first jumper is in and jumping steadily, the next player enters. Players continue to enter the game until space is filled (usually about six or seven jumpers). Then all students recite memory passage in rhythm as players jump. Play continues until all students have had a turn or until time is up.

(Variation: For easier jumping, players may jump individually.)

LISTEN UP!

Materials Checklist

◆ Bible
◆ large index cards
◆ felt pen

Preparation: On index cards, write the words and reference of the Bible Memory Passage—a short phrase on each card. Make two sets of cards.

Procedure: Arrange one set of Bible Memory Passage cards in order on the floor. Students gather around cards and read passage aloud several times to become familiar with it. Then divide class into two teams. Teams line up as in sketch. Shuffle both sets of memory passage cards together and spread all cards facedown on the floor between teams.

Assign each student a number, using the same set of numbers for each team. To begin play, call out any one of the numbers you have assigned to students. Each of the two students with this number quickly chooses a card and brings it to his or her team. Repeat process. As students bring cards to their teams, team members try to place the cards in order. If a student brings a duplicate card, player who is called next returns card to pile before choosing a new card. Team which first places all cards in order wins.

LOVE NOTE SCROLLS

Materials Checklist

◆ Bible
◆ two large sheets of paper in contrasting colors
◆ felt marker
◆ scissors
◆ yarn
◆ masking tape

Preparation: Draw a large heart on each sheet of paper; cut out hearts. Use marker to write the Bible Memory Passage on both paper hearts (sketch a). Cut each heart into eight pieces; roll each piece into a scroll and tie with yarn (sketch b). Hide scrolls around room or outdoor area.

Procedure: Divide class into two teams. Teams search for scrolls. When teams find all eight pieces of their puzzle, they assemble hearts and tape pieces together. Students read verse aloud. (*Tip:* Other shapes such as circles, stars, Easter eggs, etc. may be used.)

a.

b.

PULLED FROM THE PIT

Materials Checklist

◆ Bible
◆ three large sheets of poster board
◆ felt pen
◆ construction paper
◆ scissors
◆ masking tape

Preparation: Letter words of Bible Memory Passage on one sheet of poster board. On each remaining sheet of poster board, draw an outline of a pit. Draw lines up one side of each pit, one line for each team member. From construction paper, cut two simple outlines of a person. Attach a loop of tape to the back of each figure and secure to the bottom of each pit. Attach all three posters to wall.

Procedure: Read passage aloud with students. A teacher or volunteer stands next to each "pit." Divide group into two equal teams. Each team lines up opposite a "pit." At a signal, the first two players on each team run to their pit. They recite the passage to the teacher or helper, each player saying alternate words. If students successfully recite passage, the teacher moves the figure up to the next line on the pit. Players run back to their team and tag the next two players in line, who repeat process. Continue until all players have had a turn and the figure has been rescued from the pit. (*Variation:* Instead of rescuing the figures from pits, have figures climb ladders.)

•

TRAFFIC JAM

Materials Checklist

◆ Bible
◆ 56 large index cards
◆ four small pictures or stickers showing cars and trucks
◆ glue
◆ felt pen
◆ butcher paper or chalkboard and chalk

Preparation: Letter Bible Memory Passage on chalkboard or paper. Write the alphabet on index cards—one letter on each card. Make two sets of alphabet cards. Glue car and truck pictures to four extra index cards; place two of these in each set of alphabet cards.

Procedure: Divide the class into two teams. Give each team a set of cards to be divided as evenly as possible among team members. Teacher calls out first word of Bible Memory Passage. The players holding the letters in the word arrange themselves to correctly spell out word. If a letter is used more than once in a word, player holding card with picture may substitute it for duplicate letter. When team members think they are in the correct order, they yell "Traffic Jam!" The other team must freeze in position. If the word is spelled correctly, the team gets one point, and game continues with next word of memory passage. When all words have been spelled, team with the most points wins. For difficult or new words, ask a volunteer to tell the meaning of the word. (*Simplification:* Play game using only one verse of the passage at a time.)

ILLUSTRATED BIBLE PASSAGE

Materials Checklist

◆ Bible
◆ large sheets of butcher paper
◆ tempera paints and paintbrushes
◆ felt pens

Preparation: Letter a portion of the Bible Memory Passage across the top of each sheet of paper.

Procedure: Read passage aloud with students. Divide class into groups of two or three. Each group illustrates a portion of the passage, using paints or felt pens. Display papers in your classroom.

DISAPPEARING WORDS

Materials Checklist

◆ Bible
◆ 12 sheets of construction paper
◆ felt pens
◆ two number cubes

Preparation: Letter phrases of the Bible Memory Passage on sheets of construction paper. Number papers from 1-12. Lay papers in order in a grid on floor or table.

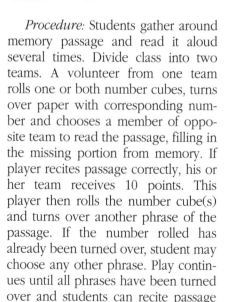

Procedure: Students gather around memory passage and read it aloud several times. Divide class into two teams. A volunteer from one team rolls one or both number cubes, turns over paper with corresponding number and chooses a member of opposite team to read the passage, filling in the missing portion from memory. If player recites passage correctly, his or her team receives 10 points. This player then rolls the number cube(s) and turns over another phrase of the passage. If the number rolled has already been turned over, student may choose any other phrase. Play continues until all phrases have been turned over and students can recite passage from memory.

CRAZY EIGHTS

Materials Checklist

◆ Bible
◆ eight metal bottle caps
◆ chalk
◆ measuring stick

Preparation: On a paved area, use chalk to draw eight large squares in various locations, at least 8 feet (2.4 m) apart. Letter the words of Bible Memory Passage in squares—one phrase in each square. Number the squares 1-8. Draw a starting line and a small circle about 10 feet (3 m) from square one.

Procedure: Players line up on start-

ing line and recite passage in unison. Teacher gently throws all the bottle caps into the air, above the circle. Players count how many bottle caps land inside the circle and race to the square with that same number. The first player to reach the square gets to stay there, while the other players return to the starting line. Players recite passage again, pausing to allow player in the square to say his or her phrase alone. Repeat process until entire passage is recited phrase by phrase. (*Note:* When tossing bottle caps results in a repeated number, another player may be added to that square.)

CLOTHESPIN PASS

Materials Checklist

For each student—
◆ clothespin
◆ slips of paper

Preparation: On slips of paper write phrases of the Bible Memory Passage, a different phrase on each paper. (There should be at least one slip of paper for each team member.) Make a complete set for each team of four or five students.

Procedure: Divide group into teams. Give a clothespin to each student. Teams line up, players standing arm's length from each other. Place one set of shuffled papers on the floor near the feet of the first person on each team. All the phrases should be visible. When teacher says "go," the first player on each team uses his or her clothespin to pick up the first phrase of the passage, then passes it to the second player, who takes it with clothespin and continues passing it. When last player receives the phrase, he or she places it on the floor, runs to the front of the line to pick up the next phrase of the passage, and begins passing the phrase down the line. Repeat procedure until one team has successfully passed the entire passage to the end of the line, put it in order and read it aloud together.

BIBLE SKULLIES

Materials Checklist

◆ Bible
◆ chalk
◆ soda bottle cap
◆ clay or play dough
◆ measuring stick

Preparation: On a paved area outdoors, use chalk to draw a 5-foot (1.5-m) square court as shown in sketch. Number squares as shown. Divide the Bible Memory Passage into 13 phrases lettered in boxes. Make a game piece (called a "loady") by filling a soda bottle cap with clay or play dough and allowing it to harden.

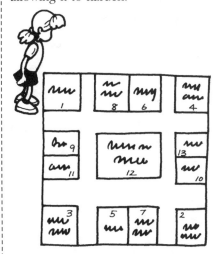

Procedure: First player kneels behind outer line of court by square one and places loady on the ground outside of court. Player then recites the first phrase of passage and tries to flick loady, smooth side down, into first square. If player succeeds, he or she may flick loady to second square and recite the first and second phrases of passage. If player misses, second player resumes where first player left off, after saying phrases played so far. Players may kneel to flick loady at any point outside of court.

Continue process until entire passage has been recited. Repeat as time allows. (*Optional:* If loady is flicked outside of court, the next player must start at the beginning.)

(*Variation:* Divide class into two teams. Players gain points each time loady lands in correct square.)

OFF-THE-WALL BALL

Materials Checklist
- ◆ Bible
- ◆ high-bounce rubber ball (such as a hand ball)
- ◆ chalk
- ◆ measuring stick

Preparation: This game requires the use of an unobstructed wall. On a paved area, use chalk to draw an 8-foot (2.4-m) square handball court extending from the base of the wall as shown in sketch. If students are unfamiliar with the Bible Memory Passage, letter it on the wall in chalk.

Procedure: Choose a volunteer to serve the ball. Other players line up near the right edge of court. The server starts the game by reciting the first word of the Bible Memory Passage, entering into the handball court and bouncing the ball once on the ground so it hits the wall. The server runs to the end of the line as the next player in line enters the court, allowing the ball to bounce on the ground once, and recites the second word of the passage before hitting the ball back to the wall for the next player. The ball must bounce only once before hitting the wall and only once before the next player can hit it. If player allows the ball to bounce on the ground more than once or hits the ball out of court or cannot recite the next word in the passage before hitting the ball, he or she proceeds to the end of the lineup. The server then starts the game and the passage over again with other players keeping their current positions in line. The object of the game is to recite the entire passage.

GLOVE PASS

Materials Checklist
- ◆ Bible
- ◆ music cassette
- ◆ index cards
- ◆ felt pens
- ◆ paper bag
- ◆ cassette player
- ◆ one gardening glove

Preparation: Letter short phrases of a Bible Memory Passage on separate index cards.

Procedure: Place index cards in order on the floor and read passage aloud with students. Then place cards in a paper bag. Students form a circle. While you play music on cassette player, students pass a gardening glove from player to player. To pass the glove, each player must put it on his or her neighbor's hand, then player takes it off and puts it on the next player. When you stop the music, player wearing the glove chooses a card from the bag. Player reads the phrase aloud and tries to complete the passage, beginning with that phrase.

HOPSCOTCH RELAY

Materials Checklist
- ◆ Bible
- ◆ two pieces of chalk
- ◆ two margarine tub lids
- ◆ paper
- ◆ tape
- ◆ felt pen

Preparation: Letter the words of the Bible Memory Passage on each of two sheets of paper and tape one paper on each lid. On outdoor paved area, use chalk to draw two identical hopscotch diagrams as shown in sketch. Place lid and chalk in last square.

Procedure: Divide class into two teams. Teams line up at hopscotch diagrams. First player from each team hops through hopscotch, hopping on one foot in single blocks and two feet in double blocks. Upon reaching last square, player leans over on one foot and picks up chalk and lid, then writes the first word of memory passage in end circle. Player returns chalk and lid to last square and hops back through hopscotch to tag the next player who repeats process, writing next word of passage in circle. The first team to complete entire memory passage and return to line wins.

SAND WRITING

Materials Checklist
- Bible
- index cards
- felt pen
- wet sand
- two large baking pans or cookie sheets
- two pencils
- newspapers

Preparation: Letter phrases of Bible Memory Passage on index cards—one phrase on each card. Make two sets. Stack each set of cards in order. Fill each baking pan or cookie sheet with wet sand. Place pans on newspapers on tables or floor (or on ground if playing outside). Place stacks of index cards faceup across room from pans (see sketch).

stack of cards

← pan of sand

Procedure: Divide class into two teams. Each team lines up next to a pan of sand. At a signal, one member of each team runs to stack, takes the top card, runs back to pan and uses pencil to write first word of phrase in sand. Team members say entire phrase aloud, then player "erases" word. Team members take turns running to get cards and writing words in sand. First team to complete process and say the entire passage is the winner.

QUICK QUOTE

Materials Checklist
- Bible
- small index cards
- felt pens
- chalkboard and chalk or butcher paper

Preparation: Letter the Bible Memory Passage on chalkboard or paper.

Procedure: Divide group into pairs. Give each pair of students index cards and a felt pen. Students copy words of memory passage, a short phrase on each card. Erase the passage from chalkboard or cover paper. Pairs shuffle their cards. When teacher says "go," pairs race to put cards back in the correct order. If time allows, remove several cards from each set and have pairs try to put them in order again.

HULA HOOP HOOPLA

Materials Checklist
- Bible
- hula hoops—one for every five or six students
- chalk or construction paper
- masking tape and felt pen

Preparation: Letter the words of Bible Memory Passage on construction paper—one or two phrases on each paper. Tape papers in various locations around the room. (If playing outside, use chalk to write phrases on the ground in different places within close proximity.)

Procedure: Divide class into teams of five or six students. Teams line up behind a designated point. First student from each team holds a hula hoop around waist. When teacher recites first phrase of passage, first student on each team runs to corresponding location. Second student from each team runs to first student and gets inside hula hoop. The pair then runs to next location as teacher recites second phrase of passage. One more student is added inside hula hoop each time a phrase of the passage is completed. When all team members are inside hoop, reverse the process, removing one person from the hoop at each phrase, until passage is completed. (*Optional:* Teams compete one at a time to see which team can run through the passage the fastest.)

BIBLE PASSAGE TANGLE

Materials Checklist

◆ large ball of yarn or string
◆ chalkboard and chalk

Preparation: Letter Bible Memory Passage on chalkboard.

Procedure: Students sit in chairs or on the floor in a circle. Read Bible Memory Passage several times with students. The first player holds the ball of yarn in one hand and the loose end of the yarn firmly with the other; then, while saying the first word of the passage, the player throws the ball of yarn across the circle to another student (while still holding the loose end of yarn). The player who catches the ball says the next word while holding the yarn strand and throwing the ball to another student. Continue until passage has been completed several times.

INVENT-A-LANGUAGE

Materials Checklist

◆ Bible
◆ chalkboard and chalk or butcher paper and felt pen

Preparation: Letter Bible Memory Passage on chalkboard or paper.

Procedure: Divide class into teams of two to three students. Assign each group a verse of the Bible Passage. Each team invents its own language by developing an imaginary rule to the English language. For example, take the last letter from a word and add it to the beginning, then add -ich to the end of the word. ("Verse" becomes "eversich.") Teacher sets a time limit and groups practice saying the Bible verse in their new language. Each group presents its verse to the class, while class tries to figure out the group's language rule.

MEMORY PASSAGE FREEZE TAG

Materials Checklist

◆ several index cards with the Bible Memory Passage written on them

Procedure: Establish boundaries and choose a student to be "It." When other players are tagged by "It," they must freeze until they repeat the Bible Memory Passage. (If a student is unable to say the passage, he or she may be given a copy of the passage to read aloud.) After successfully saying the passage, the tagged students may run freely again. At any point, teacher may yell, "Everybody freeze!" All students stop where they are, including "It." Teacher selects new "It" and game proceeds until all students have had a chance to repeat the Bible Memory Passage.

MEMORY MIX-UP

Materials Checklist

◆ Bible
◆ index cards
◆ felt pen
◆ masking tape

Preparation: Letter one word (or short phrase) of the Bible Memory Passage on each index card (sketch a). On opposite side of each card, write the name of a Bible story character or event (sketch b).

a.

| know | that | the |

b.

| David | Saul | Jonathan |

Procedure: Tape a card onto the back of each student. (Teacher keeps extra cards.) Students try to guess what names or events they have on their backs by asking yes-or-no questions of other students in the room. After student has guessed correctly, he or she takes off the card and tapes it in passage order along the wall. When all of the cards have been put in their proper places, students read the passage aloud in unison.

BIBLE WORDS BOUNCE

Materials Checklist

◆ Bible
◆ chalkboard and chalk or butcher paper
◆ felt pen and tape or tacks
◆ two basketballs or rubber balls
◆ large play area

Preparation: Letter words of Bible Memory Passage on chalkboard or paper and display.

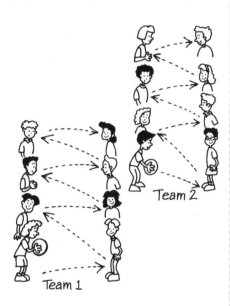

Procedure: Divide class into two teams. Each team forms two lines which stand about 8 feet (2.4 m) apart, facing each other (see sketch). Teams practice bounce-passing ball back and forth between lines. At a signal, teams compete to pass ball, saying a word of the passage with each bounce. Remove passage poster, then play game several more times.

GROUP EFFORT

Materials Checklist

◆ large sheet of paper
◆ felt pens

Preparation: Letter Bible Memory Passage on sheet of paper. Divide passage into three or four sections by lettering each section with a different color felt pen.

Procedure: Divide class into three or four groups. Assign each group a section (color) of the Bible Memory Passage. Beginning slowly, point to groups one at a time to have them stand and recite their section of the passage. Repeat several times, increasing speed. Finally, take the sheet of paper away.

(Variation: Have students do an action illustrating their section of the passage while saying it.)

BIBLE PASSAGE POP-UP

Materials Checklist

◆ Bible
◆ index cards
◆ felt pen
◆ stopwatch or watch with a second hand

Preparation: Letter words of Bible Memory Passage on index cards—one phrase on each card.

Procedure: Distribute memory passage cards, one or two cards to each student. Sitting in a circle, students recite the passage, each student in turn "popping up" (quickly standing) and saying the phrase on his or her card. Use stopwatch or watch to determine how quickly the group recites the passage using the pop-up method. Students exchange cards and attempt to beat their former time.

SHORT ORDER BIBLE PASSAGE

Materials Checklist
- ◆ Bible
- ◆ large index cards
- ◆ felt pen

Preparation: Letter Bible Memory Passage on index cards—one word on each card. Make two sets of cards. Mix up the cards within each set.

Procedure: Divide class into two teams. Distribute one set of cards among the players of each team. To begin play, read a phrase (four to six words) from Bible Memory Passage. Team members holding cards with the words of the phrase quickly move to the front of the room and arrange themselves in order (see sketch). When cards are in order, team members not holding cards read the phrase aloud. The team that completes this procedure first is the winner of that round. Repeat game using different phrases each time. (*Optional:* Increase the difficulty of the game by using longer phrases.)

BIBLE BALLOON BOP

Materials Checklist
- ◆ several inflated balloons

Procedure: Class stands in a circle, or on opposite sides of a line as in volleyball (for team play). A balloon is set in motion and bopped around the circle or back and forth across the line. The first player to hit the balloon says the first word of the Bible Memory Passage. The second player to hit the balloon says the second word and so on. If the balloon hits the ground, the opposite team wins a point. If a player cannot say his or her word, the opposite team wins a point. To vary the game, players can say one, two or three words of the passage at a time.

WRITING RELAY

Materials Checklist
- ◆ Bibles
- ◆ masking tape
- ◆ chalkboard and chalk

Preparation: Letter the reference for the Bible Memory Passage on chalkboard. Use masking tape to mark a line on the floor at least 15 feet (4.5 m) from chalkboard.

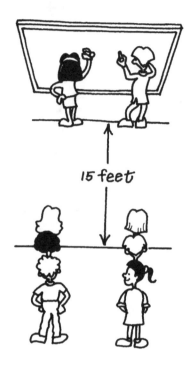

15 feet

Procedure: Review the Bible Memory Passage with students. Divide class into two or more teams. Each team lines up behind designated line. At a signal, the first member of each team runs to the chalkboard and writes the first word of the Bible Memory Passage, runs back to the line and passes the chalk to the next member of the team who writes the second word. If a mistake has been made, a player may use his or her turn to correct the mistake. Play continues until one team has written the complete passage correctly and all members are seated on the floor to show that they are finished. (*Variation:* Have players hop on one foot to the chalkboard or walk backwards.)

FRIENDLY FEUD QUIZ GAME

Materials Checklist
- index cards and pen
- table
- game bell
- chalkboard and chalk

Preparation: On index cards, letter questions (can include questions for Bible story review, life application and Bible Memory Passage review).

Procedure: Divide class into two teams that sit in rows facing each other. Place the game bell on a table between the two rows.

The first player from each team stands with one hand on the table and one hand behind his or her back. Read aloud the question on the first card. The first person to ring the bell may answer the question for ten points; if answer is wrong, the other player may answer it, winning five points for his or her team. If neither contestant gets the answer, put the question at the bottom of the pile to be asked later. Repeat procedure until all players have had several turns. Keep score on the chalkboard.

THAT'S THE WAY IT WAS

Materials Checklist
- slips of paper
- pen
- chair for each student except one

Preparation: Choose words that are repeated several times in the lesson's Bible story; write each word on a slip of paper—one slip of paper for each student. (Words may be repeated.) Place chairs in a circle.

Procedure: Students sit in circle; one student stands in the middle of the circle. Give one slip of paper to each seated student. To play, read or tell the Bible story with expression. Each time you say a word that is on a slip of paper, the student holding that slip must stand, turn around and sit down again in the same chair. Meanwhile, the player in the middle tries to sit on the chair before the student sits down. If the player in the middle succeeds, the student without a seat becomes the player in the middle and gives his or her slip to the student now seated. Continue telling the story.

(*Variation:* For a challenge, insert the phrase "That's the way it was!" at various times during the story. Whenever you say this phrase, all students must stand and find a new seat. The player in the middle can use this opportunity to find a seat. The student left without a seat after the scramble will be the player in the middle as you continue to read the story.)

BALLOON POP

Materials Checklist
- Bible
- small strips of paper
- pen
- balloons
- large plastic garbage bags

Preparation: List 10 events from the Bible story, one event on each strip of paper (see sketch). Make an identical set of story strips for each team of six to eight students. Roll strips and insert one into each balloon. Inflate and tie balloons. Put each set of 10 balloons into a large plastic bag.

> Jesus talks to a lawyer.

> Jesus tells a story.

> Jewish man takes a trip.

> Robbers beat Jewish man.

> Jewish man waits for help.

> Priest ignores man.

> Levite ignores man.

> Samaritan bandages man's cuts.

> Samaritan takes man to inn.

> Jesus tells lawyer, "Be kind like the Samaritan."

Procedure: Divide class into teams of six to eight students each. Give each team a plastic bag with balloons. At your signal, teams race to remove balloons from bag, pop them and put the Bible story events in the correct sequence. After all teams have put their strips in order, discuss the Bible story by asking questions.

REBUS REVIEW

Materials Checklist

◆ Bible
◆ pen
◆ one strip of paper for each student
◆ chalkboard and chalk or large sheet of butcher paper

Preparation: On strips of paper, list statements about events in the Bible story—one statement for each student.

Procedure: Give each player a paper strip. Students silently read statements and think of a symbol or drawing that represents the Bible story event. Teacher calls on individual students to draw their symbol on the chalkboard or paper. Students take turns guessing what each person's symbol means. Players can draw more than one symbol if necessary; however, the goal is to communicate the event in as few symbols as possible.

After each event is guessed, ask questions that review the Bible story or help students apply the Bible truth to their lives.

QUESTION CUBE

Materials Checklist

◆ square box (6x6 inches [15x15 cm] or larger)
◆ felt pens
◆ butcher paper
◆ scissors
◆ chalkboard and chalk
◆ tape
◆ glue

Preparation: If necessary, cover box with butcher paper. On the sides of the box, write the following words, one on each side: "Who?," "What?," "When?," "Where?," "Why?," "Free points!"

Procedure: Divide class into two teams. A volunteer from Team A rolls the question cube and uses the word that lands faceup in a question about the Bible story. For example, "Why did the son want to leave his father's home?"

Players on Team B who want to answer the question stand up quickly. The first player to stand may answer for his or her team. For each correct answer, the team is given ten points. Keep score on a chalkboard.

If your students have difficulty coming up with questions, you may want to have a list of prepared questions from which to choose.

BALL TOSS

Materials Checklist

◆ Bible
◆ three baskets (or boxes)
◆ index cards
◆ felt pen
◆ softball (or beanbag)
◆ tape
◆ large sheet of paper or chalkboard and chalk

Preparation: Label three index cards: "True," "False," and "Not in Story"; attach each card to a basket. On more index cards, write statements about the Bible story that can be identified as "true" or "false"—at least one card for each student. Include several statements which do not relate to the story.

Procedure: Divide class into two teams. Teams line up 6-8 feet (1.8-2.4 m) from the three baskets. One student acts as scorekeeper. First player on one team chooses a card and reads the statement. Player identifies the statement as true, false or not in story, then attempts to toss the ball into the correct basket. Player receives five points for stating the correct answer and five points if the ball lands in the basket. If the answer is incorrect, anyone may correct the statement, and the player may still earn five points by tossing ball into the correct basket. Teams take turns. Question cards may be reused. Scorekeeper records each team's score on paper or chalkboard.

THREE-LEGGED CHICKEN GAME

Materials Checklist
◆ Bible
◆ two chairs
◆ paper
◆ pen
◆ two large index cards
◆ strips of cloth
   (one for every two students)
◆ tape

Preparation: On a sheet of paper, list true-or-false statements about events in the Bible story; at least one statement for every two students in your group. Label one index card "True" and another "False." Tape labeled index cards to chairs placed opposite each other between teams (sketch a).

Procedure: Divide class into two equal teams. (If you have an extra student, he or she may read aloud the statements.) Each team divides into pairs. Pairs use clean cloth strips to tie inside legs together above the knee (sketch b). Pairs are assigned numbers. Teams sit on floor as shown in sketch a.

After teams are seated, leader reads aloud a statement and calls out a number. The pairs with that number jump up and run to sit in the "true" or "false" chair. The pair of players who sit in the correct chair first score a point for their team. In case of a tie, each team scores a point. Repeat process until all statements have been read. Pause to allow students to correct each false statement.

CHAIR SCRAMBLE

Materials Checklist
◆ Bible
◆ four chairs
◆ paper
◆ pencil
◆ large index cards
◆ tape

Preparation: On a sheet of paper, list true-or-false statements about events in the Bible story, at least one statement for every two students in your group. Label two index cards "True" and two cards "False." Tape labeled index cards to chairs (sketch a). Place both sets of chairs at opposite ends of playing area.

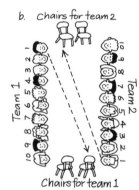

Procedure: Divide class into two equal teams. (If you have an extra student, he or she may read aloud the true or false statements.) Teams sit on floor as shown in sketch a. Assign each student a number (sketch b).

To play, leader reads aloud a statement and calls out a number. The students from each team with that number jump up and run to sit in their team's "true" or "false" chair. The student who sits in the correct chair first scores a point for his or her team. In case of a tie, each team scores a point. Repeat process until all true or false statements have been read. Pause to allow students to correct each false statement. Repeat game as time permits.

QUICK DRAW

Materials Checklist
◆ Bible
◆ at least 10 small slips of paper
◆ pen
◆ chair
◆ chalkboard and chalk
   or two large pads of paper
   and two felt pens

Preparation: On slips of paper write 10 or more words or phrases from the Bible story.

Procedure: Divide class into two teams. Team sits on the floor as far away from each other as possible. Teams each choose one artist and one runner. Place chair between teams (see sketch). Leader stands in front near chalkboard or paper. At your signal, artist from each team runs up to the front and reads a slip of paper that leader is holding. Players quickly draw a picture of the word or phrase, without speaking or drawing letters or words. Teams try to secretly guess the correct word or phrase. When a team has the correct answer, team runner quickly runs and sits in the chair and calls out word or phrase. Team gets one point and play starts over again. Teams choose a different artist and runner each time. When all words have been drawn, team with the most points wins.

BALLOON BUST

Materials Checklist

◆ music cassette
◆ cassette player
◆ beanbag or sponge ball
◆ balloons
◆ tape
◆ paper
◆ pencil
◆ chair for each student

Preparation: Arrange chairs in a circle. On small slips of paper, write statements from the Bible story, leaving out one key word in each statement. Make one slip of paper for each student; place each one inside a balloon. Inflate balloons and attach to chairs with tape.

Procedure: Students sit in chairs. As cassette is played, students toss beanbag randomly around or across the circle. When the music stops, whoever has the beanbag pops the balloon taped to his or her chair and reads the sentence, filling in the blank. Play continues until all the balloons have been popped. (If a student has already popped his or her balloon and is left holding the beanbag, it should be passed to another student.)

CHOPSTICKS RELAY

Materials Checklist

◆ Bible
◆ two large bowls
◆ three Chinese take-out food containers
◆ felt pen
◆ paper
◆ pencil
◆ table
◆ chalkboard and chalk or large sheet of paper

For each student—

◆ Ping-Pong ball or large marshmallow
◆ set of chopsticks

Preparation: On paper, list true-or-false statements about events in the Bible story—one statement for every two students. Include several statements which do not relate to the story. Label one container "True," one "False," and one "Not in Story" (sketch a). Place an even amount of Ping-Pong balls in each bowl. Place containers on table at one side of room, bowls on the floor across the room.

Procedure: Divide class into two equal teams. (If you have an extra student, he or she may read aloud the statements and keep score.) Teams line up between bowls and containers as shown in sketch b. Give each player a set of chopsticks.

Teacher reads aloud one statement and says, "Go!" Player at the head of each line uses chopsticks to pick up a Ping-Pong ball. (Use marshmallows if balls are difficult for your students to handle.) He or she then passes ball to next player with chopsticks. Ball is passed most effectively if it rests on top of chopsticks (sketch c). Procedure continues until ball reaches the end of the line. The last player carries the ball with the chopsticks and drops it into the appropriate food container. Player then goes to the head of the line. The first student to put the ball in the correct container scores a point for his or her team. Repeat process until all players have had a turn. Teacher records each team's score on chalkboard or paper.

a.

b.

c.

TIMER TALES

Materials Checklist

◆ kitchen timer or watch that indicates seconds

Procedure: Students sit in a circle. Set timer for 15 seconds as the first student begins telling the Bible story. When the timer rings, the first student must stop mid-sentence, and the second student picks up where the first left off. Reset the timer. Storytelling continues in this manner until the complete story is told. (*Variation:* Have students create a modern version of the Bible story using present-day people and situations.)

ACTiONARY

Materials Checklist
- large box or chest
- variety of items to use as props
  in skits (loaf of bread, purse, hat, pan, bandage, base-ball bat, doll, Bible, stationery, etc.)

Procedure: Allow each student to choose an item from the box. Students work in groups of two or three to compose and perform short skits to illustrate the principle learned in that day's lesson. The items chosen from the box must be used in the skit.

TAKE MY ADVICE

Materials Checklist
- paper
- pencil

Preparation: On a sheet of paper, write several real-life situations in which students might or might not follow advice given. (Examples: 1. Your mom asks you to call if you're going to be late coming home. 2. Your teacher tells you to study for a test. 3. Your coach tells you to keep your eye on the ball. 4. Your dad tells you to save some of your allowance each week.)

Procedure: Read the first situation aloud to the group. Ask a few volunteers to act out what might happen if the advice is followed. Then ask other volunteers to act out what might happen if the advice is not followed. Repeat process using several situations.

WINNERS' CIRCLE

Materials Checklist
- music cassette and cassette player
- index card for each student
- felt pen
- masking tape or chalk

Preparation: Divide cards into three equal sets. Write actions related to your lesson such as "share," "be kind," "forgive" and "be patient" on one set of index cards—one word or phrase on each card. (If necessary, you may make duplicates.) Write a location on each of the second set of cards (i.e., classroom, home, store, playground, bus, car, kitchen, bedroom, backyard, park, beach, swimming pool). Write a person on each of the third set of cards (i.e., boy, girl, baby, mom, dad, grandma, neighbor, five-year-old child, teenager, teacher). Use masking tape or chalk to create three large, concentric circles on the floor (see sketch). On the large circles, mark one small square for each student to stand in, spacing squares evenly around circles. Mark an *X* on three of the squares as in sketch.

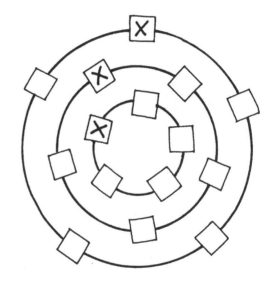

Procedure: Divide class into three equal teams. Team one stands on squares in outer circle. Team two stands on squares in center circle and so on. Players on the outer circle receive index cards with locations; players in the middle circle receive cards with people; players in the inner circle receive action cards. As cassette is played, students move clockwise around circles from square to square. When the music stops, students on the boxes marked *X* read the information on their cards. The first player to raise his or her hand may use all the information on the three cards to tell how a person might obey God. (For example, "Mom was patient when she had to wait in line at the store.") Player's team receives a point. The first team to earn five points is the winning circle.

SOCK PASS

Materials Checklist

◆ one sock for each team

Procedure: Two or more teams line up single file. A sock is given to the first person on each team. When the leader gives a signal, teams compete to pass the sock from one member to the next down the line. Each player may allow only one hand to touch the sock and sock must be pulled tightly over each player's hand before it is a legal pass (see sketch).

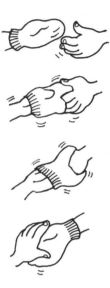

NAMES OF FAME

Materials Checklist

◆ blank label for each student
◆ felt pen

Preparation: On each label, write the name of a famous person your students are sure to be familiar with.

Procedure: Attach one label to the back of each student's shirt. Students mingle with classmates, asking questions to determine whose names are on their backs. Only questions that can be answered yes or no are allowed. For example: "Am I a woman?" "Am I an actor?" "Am I Bill Cosby?"

THREE-TEAM TUG-OF-WAR

Materials Checklist

◆ three scraps of cloth
◆ two or three ropes

Procedure: Tie two or three ropes together to form a three-handled rope (see sketch). Make sure the knot is tied securely and will not pull apart during the game. Divide class into three teams. Each team assembles, holding onto one of the three ropes, as in a standard tug-of-war game. Mark three spots on the ground with scraps of cloth (see sketch). Each team competes to pull the knot in the rope over its spot.

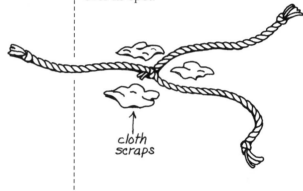

cloth
scraps

GORELKI

(Russian Line Tag)

Materials Checklist

◆ rope or masking tape

Procedure: Choose one player to be "It." Divide group into two teams. Teams line up in pairs as shown in sketch. Mark a line about 10 feet (3 m) from the front of the line. "It" stands behind line. When "It" says, "Last pair run," the last pair runs up the outside of their lines and joins hands at the front of the lines before "It" can tag either one of them. If "It" tags a player, tagged player becomes the new "It" and they switch places.

CRAZY HIGHWAY

(This game works best with six to eight players.)

Materials Checklist

◆ chalk

Procedure: Choose one player to be the "Painter." On outdoor paved area, players stand in a line behind Painter. Painter uses chalk to mark an X on the ground, turns around and begins to walk backwards, dragging the chalk along the pavement to make a "crazy highway." First player counts to 10 and then begins to follow the highway wherever it leads. Each consecutive player counts to 10, then follows the player in front of him or her. As players get closer to Painter, the Painter may intersect the line, creating a second X. First player to reach X must get off the highway line and start again from the first X. If the Painter intersects the line again, then the second player must stop and return to the first X. Once a player is back on the highway, he or she does not have to stop at any more intersections. In this way, a player only has to stop at an intersection once. This sequence continues until a player is able to tag the Painter. The player who tags the Painter becomes the new Painter and game begins again.

SILLY SENTENCES MIXER

Materials Checklist

◆ envelope and two index cards for each student

◆ felt pen

Preparation: Write the first part of a true statement on one index card. Write the second part of the statement on another index card. Make a set of two cards for each student (see sketch for some examples).

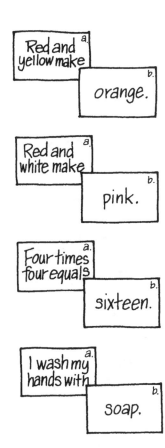

Mix up cards. Place a mismatched set of cards in each envelope, making sure each set contains one *a* and one *b* card.

Procedure: Distribute one envelope to each student. Students mingle and exchange cards until everyone has a matched statement.

STREETS AND ALLEYS

(This game works best with at least 20 students.)

Materials Checklist

◆ chalk or rope

Preparation: Use chalk or rope to make a home base on outdoor playing field (see sketch).

Procedure: Choose one player to be "It" and another player to be the "Chaser." Remaining players line up side by side in a grid pattern, linking hands to form at least four separate "streets" consisting of at least four players each (see sketch).

"It" and "Chaser" stand facing streets, opposite from home base (see sketch). Game begins when teacher calls out "Streets!" "It" runs to home base weaving through the lines (streets), while "Chaser" tries to tag him or her. However, when the leader calls out "Alleys!" all players drop hands, make a quarter turn to the right, and join hands with new players on either side. This turns the "streets" into "alleys." "It" now has to run in a new direction to get to home base. Leader continues to call out "Streets!" and "Alleys!" to make the game unpredictable. If "It" reaches home base without being tagged, he or she may choose another player to be the new "It." But if "Chaser" tags "It" then "Chaser" becomes the new "It."

BETWEEN THE KNEES RELAY

Materials Checklist

◆ large ball for each team
◆ masking tape or rope (for goal line)

Procedure: Divide group into even teams, with six or fewer players on each team. Each team forms a line in a large playing area. The first player on each team places the ball between his or her knees and runs (or hops) to a goal line 30 feet (9 m) away. After crossing the line, the player grabs the ball and runs back to the team, hands ball to the next player, who places it between knees and hops toward goal line. Continue relay until everyone on the team has run.

RED LIGHT, GREEN LIGHT

Materials Checklist

◆ chalk or tape
◆ measuring stick

Preparation: Use chalk or tape to make a starting line and a finish line, at least 15 feet (4.5 m) apart.

Procedure: Choose one player to be "It." "It" stands behind the finish line. Players stand behind starting line. Game begins when "It" turns his or her back to the players and calls "green light!" Players then run towards the finish line. When "It" calls "red light," players must stop running and freeze in position. "It" turns around to face the runners and tries to catch someone moving. "It" may send anyone caught moving back to the starting line. Game continues until one runner is close enough to tag "It." The player that tags "It" becomes the new "It." (The closer the runners get to the finish line, the quicker the intervals are between "green light" and "red light.")

FORCEBALL

(British or Australian Ball Game)

Materials Checklist

◆ one basketball or kick ball
◆ chalk or masking tape
◆ measuring stick

Preparation: Use chalk or tape to make two parallel lines about 3 yards (2.7 m) apart.

Procedure: Divide group into two teams. Players line up on lines, side by side with legs apart and feet touching as shown in sketch. Teams face each other. The object of the game is to roll the ball between the legs of the players on the opposing team. Players bat the ball to the opposite team using only their hands. Players cannot move their feet. Teams get one point every time the ball rolls through the opposing team's legs. Team with the most points wins the game.

EGYPTIAN STICK RACE

Materials Checklist

◆ one 4-foot (1.2-m) stick for each player

Procedure: Players stand in a large circle about 8 feet (2.4 m) apart from each other. Each player faces the middle of the circle and holds a stick upright, in the left hand, with one end on the ground. At teacher's signal, each player lets go of his or her own stick and races to catch the stick of the player to the right, before it touches the ground. If the stick touches the ground, the player who failed to catch it is out, along with the stick. (Play a practice round first, until students feel confident.) Circle shrinks in size as more and more players are out. Last player remaining in the game is the winner.

UP AND AWAY

Materials Checklist

◆ ten balloons of equal shape and size
◆ two large containers (baskets or boxes)
◆ felt pen

Preparation: Blow up balloons. Write the numbers 1 through 10 on the balloons—one number on each balloon. Place containers at opposite sides of playing area.

Procedure: Divide group into two teams. Toss balloons into air. The object of the game is for each team to get the higher-numbered balloons into its container, without using hands. Elbows, heads and feet may be used. Each balloon is worth the number of points written on it. The winning team is the one scoring the most points.

CANOE RACES

Materials Checklist

- four large sheets of cardboard
- craft knife
- heavy-duty stapler
- staples or strapping tape
- broad felt marker
- rope or masking tape for goal line

Preparation: Draw a canoe shape on each sheet of cardboard (see sketch); cut out canoe shapes. Fasten ends together to make two canoes that are open at the bottom. Make goal line 20-30 feet (6-9 m) away from starting line. Place canoes at start line.

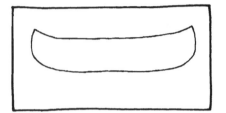

Procedure: Divide group into two teams. Each team lines up behind its canoe. At a given signal, three players climb into their canoe, hold onto the sides, race to the finish line, turn and race back to the starting line. Players climb out of canoe, next three players climb in and repeat process.

STEPPING STONES

Materials Checklist

- masking tape or rope (for goal line)
- 16-inch (40-cm) squares of heavy cloth or carpet samples—two for each team

Preparation: Mark start goal lines about 30 feet (9 m) apart.

Procedure: Divide group into teams of four to six players. Teams line up behind start line. Give the first player in each line two squares of cloth or carpet. At a given signal, the first player on each team tries to cross the goal line without his or her feet touching the ground. (Players place one square on the ground in front of them, jump on it, place the second square a few feet ahead and jump on it, pick up the first square and place it ahead, etc.). When goal line is reached, players pick up squares, run back to team and hand squares to next players, who follows the same procedure. Continue playing until all players on one team have had a turn.

HIKING BOOT RELAY

Materials Checklist

- four to eight paper bags
- two to four chairs
- chalk or masking tape

Optional—

- hats, gloves and/or large jackets

Preparation: Use chalk or masking tape to mark a starting line. For each team, place a chair 20 feet (6 m) away from the starting line.

Procedure: Divide group into teams. Each team lines up behind the starting line. Give the first player on each team two paper bags. At the signal, players put paper bags on their feet as boots, run to and around the chairs, and return to their lines, where they take off their boots and give them to the second players, who don the boots and repeat the process. The first player on each team goes to the end of his or her line. Continue playing until all members on each team have had a turn. Each player *must* run around the chair and back with the boots on his or her feet, no matter how tattered the boots become. (*Optional:* Players put on additional items such as hats, gloves and/or jackets.)

TEACHERS' BEST IDEAS

This section includes ideas to enhance and enrich any curriculum. Many were submitted by outstanding teachers across the country.

YOU'LL FIND:

- ☞ ideas to help create a sense of identity and community among your fifth and sixth graders;
- ☞ ideas to help students learn to appreciate who they are and accept others as they are;
- ☞ ways to combat the doldrums and motivate enthusiastic participation in the class;
- ☞ great learning activities;
- ☞ ideas for special clubs, parties and bulletin boards.

We hope these ideas will spark your own creativity!

INTRODUCTION, PLEASE

Divide class into pairs. Pairs must find out each other's first and middle names and one activity each likes to do. Then students take turns introducing their partners.

CLASS SLOGAN

As a class, design a slogan that expresses your class's attitude towards learning about God and/or serving God. (Example: We Practice Praise.) Make a sign to put up in your classroom or posters to put around the church campus to advertise the class.

NAME YOUR ROOM

Kids suggest and vote on names for the room or class. Make a sign with that name, cover it with clear Con-Tact® paper, and mount it on the door. Other places the classroom name could be used are in a monthly newsletter, announcements in church bulletins, service project announcements, or on T-shirts.

TWO TRUTHS AND A LIE

Students take turns telling the group three statements about themselves. Two of the statements should be true and one should be false. The rest of the group writes down the number of the statement they think is false, then volunteers may explain why they think a statement is false. Then the student reveals the false statement, and students check to see who guessed correctly.

WALKING IN YOUR FOOTSTEPS

Discuss how the phrase, "walking in someone's footsteps" means to do something like someone else does. Cut out a pair of foot outlines and place in the center of a circle. "It" stands on footprints, holding an inflated balloon. It closes eyes, spins around three times; and then bats balloon out towards circle. The person closest to where the balloon lands picks it up. It then completes the sentence, "I would follow in your footsteps by...," filling in the blank with an admirable quality of the person holding the balloon (such as, "being a good listener"). Person holding balloon then becomes It.

GROUP GETAWAY

Assist students in planning their own one-night retreat to be held at the church facility. Students select their own theme and plan activities, including menus for dinner and breakfast, as well as games, songs, and entertainment. Students may even select a member of the church as a special speaker for their retreat.

Tip:

Fifth and sixth graders are quite capable of planning their own events as long as they have guidance. Have several ideas of themes or goals ready to present to students during the planning stage. As a group, make a list of all of the students' favorite games and songs, then help students select an appropriate number of games and songs that go with the chosen theme.

MAKE-A-FRIEND BINGO

At the top of a length of butcher paper, write "Someone who...." Then, write a list of characteristics underneath, such as: has brown hair, owns a cat, likes to read. Display list. Give each student a paper with a five-by-five-square grid drawn on it. Students select phrases from the list and write one inside each box. Next, students find another student with a characteristic that matches one in their box, and asks the student to initial the box. The first student to get initials in a row, up, down, or diagonally, is the winner.

FAVORITE JOKE OR RIDDLE DAY

Have a special day when students may share a joke or riddle with the entire class at the end of class time.

Tip:

This activity can help students learn that humor can be enjoyable without being destructive. When setting up the guidelines for the types of jokes and riddles that are appropriate, discuss the difference between humor that can build us up or help us laugh at ourselves and humor that makes fun of a particular person or type of people. Also, supply students with joke and riddle books and give your own examples of good humor.

TEACHER FOR A DAY

Allow several students the opportunity to teach the class for a few minutes. They might teach a song or game, provide information on a specific subject or share a skill they have. Discuss what makes a good teacher and what makes a good learner.

PRAYER NOTEBOOK

Students write their prayer requests or praises on slips of paper and put them in a bowl. During prayer time, students take turns pulling slips of paper out of the bowl and praying the prayer requests or praises.

Then, glue prayer requests on blank sheets of notebook paper and put in a notebook. The following week, follow up on prayer requests by asking students to share how God answered their prayer requests.

PRAYER TREE

Make a prayer tree by sticking a defoliated tree branch in a flower pot. Pack dirt around branch in pot to hold the branch steady. Decorate the tree with bows, ribbons, and fake flowers. Leave the tree in an unobtrusive area. Students may make prayer requests by writing the requests on slips of paper and attaching them to the tree with yarn. Answers to prayers may be written on the backs of the prayer requests and put into a prayer box.

Tips:
1. Make sure use of the tree can be completely anonymous if the student wishes. Check the tree on a regular basis, and pray for your students' needs.
2. Prayer requests on the tree may be used during prayer time.
3. Students may wish to select a prayer request on the tree and pray about it during the week.

SURPRISE! IT'S YOU!

Students stand in a circle. Say a compliment for one of the students in the class, without using the student's name or gender. (For example: "This person was very helpful to a visitor we had in our class one day.") Then toss a beanbag or ball to the student saying "Surprise! It's you!" That student then repeats activity, selecting another student in the group to compliment.

Tip:
Instruct students to make sure each person in the group (including yourself) receives two compliments. This way, there will be suspense about who the compliment is for.

SECRET PAL PRESENTS

Each student selects a Secret Pal's name from slips of paper in a bowl. During the week, students collect items for their Secret Pal, then bring in their Secret Pal presents marked with Secret Pal's name.

Tips:
1. Students should be encouraged to put time and creativity into their presents, rather than money. Items to put in presents might be: A poem that is copied from a book and illustrated. Homemade bookmarks with Bible verses written on them. A note of encouragement. A picture. A tape of a song sung by the student. A postcard. Index cards with favorite jokes written on them. A book review. A special rock or shell. Homemade jewelry or cookies.
2. Select the names of students in another class as Secret Pals. Then surprise them with the presents the following week.

DESIGN YOUR OWN T-SHIRT CONTEST

Students design T-shirts based on a selected theme. Provide a variety of materials such as fabric scraps, ribbons, rickrack, braid and fabric paints for decorating T-shirts. Display completed T-shirts for members of congregation to see, or plan a day for students to wear T-shirts.

WHERE ARE WE?

Put a map of your area on a bulletin board marked with where each student lives and your church's location.

Students answer the following questions: **Which student in our class lives closest to the church? Which student lives the farthest from church? Which student(s) live closest to you? Which student(s) live the farthest from you? Which student(s) could you visit during the week? What is your favorite thing to see as you are on your way to church?** Pray together with your students thanking God for new friends, old friends, and beautiful things to see!

CLASS PICTURES

1. Take fun group pictures of students to display in the classroom or on a church bulletin board. Supply students with hats, sunglasses, scarves or other interesting accessories to wear in the picture.

2. Take pictures of kids posing with an empty picture frame. Use interesting backgrounds for pictures such as in front of a stained glass window, near a bouquet of flowers, at a park, a vista overlooking part of the city. Or select different places and ways for students to pose such as standing behind the pulpit, sitting up in a tree, sitting at a picnic table, lying on the ground in wheel formation (take picture from the top looking down, see sketch), kneeling in a pyramid format, going up or down a staircase, or on playground equipment. Display pictures in classroom.

Tip:

Take pictures several times throughout the year. Students will enjoy seeing how they have changed.

CLASS BANNER

Use one of the following ideas to create a banner that reflects the names and personalities of each member of the class. Hang banner as a classroom decoration or in a church hallway.

Tip:

Squares can be made from paper and taped together. Or squares can be made from fabric and sewn together to make a banner.

1. What's in a Name?

Provide students with materials to research the meaning of their first names. On an individual square, each student draws a picture depicting the meaning of his or her name.

2. Name Shapes

Students fold a square of paper in half. Using a sharp pencil, students write name along folded edge, pressing hard. Student opens paper and an impression of his or her name should be on each side. Using a black pen or crayon, students copy over impression on both sides of crease. (See sketch.) Students color in resulting spaces. (If using fabric, students write name on piece of paper. Fold a piece of tracing paper and place it inside a folded fabric square. Place name along fold and go over it with a tracing wheel. Students open fabric square and connect tracing dots with fabric paints.)

3. Bi-Colored Banner

Select two colors of paper; distribute colors evenly among students. Students use alternate color construction paper from square to cut out letters for names and simple symbols which tell about themselves. Put squares together alternating colors. (See sketch.)

4. Symbols of Us

Each student designs and makes a symbol that represents him- or herself. (See sketch for ideas.) Symbols are glued onto a banner background with the class name at the top.

Cat-owning soccer player   Ballet dancer and artist   Ball player and musician

PARENT NIGHT

Every few months, hold a special night when students and their families come together for a time of fun and getting acquainted. Hold the events in the homes of parents, at church, or at a local restaurant. Have a different theme for each quarter meeting.

Game Night

Each family brings a favorite board game. Games are set up at different tables. Assign teams, mixing up family members. Each team is given 5 to 15 minutes to play the game at their table before rotating to the next table to play the next game. (To add to the fun, teams leave games in progress, so that the next team must pick up where they left off.)

Cake Night

Each family brings an un-iced cake. Provide families with icing and decorations (such as small candies, licorice strips, marshmallows, chocolate chips, confetti, etc.). Families decorate cakes to symbolize one of their favorite activities or memories. When cakes are completed, families share what cake is about. Cakes are eaten as refreshments. (Be sure to photograph this event for your scrapbook.)

"You Are There" Night

Select a historical time or a part of the world. Families bring potluck foods that fit the theme. Provide crepe paper, construction paper and other items that families may use to make room decorations. Once the room is decorated, enjoy a potluck supper followed by several games that represent the theme. Your group may even enjoy singing some songs that go with the theme. (For example: Have a sing-a-long for an Old Fashioned Picnic Theme! Or put up some tents for a Bible Times Barbecue!) Families may even enjoy dressing up for the event.

Funniest Church Videos Contest

Families bring in their personal videos of events that have taken place at the church, in which the students were involved. The entire group votes on which video is the best. Award the winning family with a blank video cassette.

Tip:

Have families deliver their video tapes to the church ahead of time. Copy the videos onto one tape.

ROUND ROBIN LETTER

Write a letter to your students incorporating one to three questions that each student will answer. In the letter, instruct the students to write their answers at the bottom of the letter, then select another student to give the letter to. The last student to receive the letter sends it back to you. Share the completed letter with your class.

Other Ideas

1. Send a letter to each student. Enclose a self-addressed, stamped envelope, and request that the student write you in return, answering your questions at the bottom of your letter.
2. Instead of mailing a letter, mail a cassette tape. Students record their answers to your questions on the tape. Or give each student a blank cassette and request that they tape a letter to you on the cassette and return the cassette to you the following week. Listen to each student's recorded letter, and answer it on the same tape, giving the tape back to the student the following week.
3. If all your students have access to the Internet, E-mail a letter with questions to the first student along with a list of the other students in the class and their E-mail addresses. The first student adds to the letter, including an answer to your questions, then E-mails the letter to the next student on the list. The last student E-mails the letter back to you.

Question Suggestions

1. What is your favorite thing to do in the evening?
2. If you could go anywhere in the world, where would you go? Why?
3. What makes a person a good friend?
4. Suppose you were able to plan the best and most fantastic party. What kind of food would you serve? What would people do at your party? Where would you have your party? What would you celebrate at your party?
5. Who do you think is the most important person in the world? Why?
6. What is the best thing about each person in your family?
7. If you could have any animal in the world as a pet, what animal would it be? Why?
8. If you had three wishes, what would you wish for?
9. Which is your favorite room in the house? What makes it better than the other rooms?
10. If you could be any age, what age would it be? Why?

BIBLE BREAKFAST CLUB

Students meet together for breakfast before class.

Tips:

1. Breakfast could be served at church. Or set up a car pooling system and meet at different students' homes or restaurants.
2. Entice students to join the club by distributing flyers beforehand. Include trivia questions to stimulate students' curiosity.

Contributed by Vicki Wiley, Cornerstone Bible Church, Glendora, CA; and Jennifer Tebbutt, Alliance Bible Church, Hillsboro, OR

SPECIAL EVENTS

Celebrate obscure holidays or goofy national days, such as National Pickle Week or Banana Awareness Day. You may even want to make up a new one for your class, such as Mystery Bible Character Day (students come dressed as Bible characters).

C.L.U.B. T.R.U.S.T.

(**C**hildren **L**earning to **U**nderstand the **B**ible **T**hrough **R**egular **U**ninterrupted **S**tudy **T**ime) Students agree to read the Bible for at least seven minutes each day. Provide a weekly reading list of Bible passages plus questions about the passages for students to answer. Collect completed lists and pass out new lists and questions each Sunday.

Contributed by Vicki Wiley, Cornerstone Bible Church, Glendora, CA

SIMCHAT TORAH

On or around the Jewish Celebration of Simchat Torah, plan a class party to celebrate the Bible. Play Bible games, write thank-you notes to God for the Bible, and read Bible verses that emphasize the importance and value of the Bible.

Background:

In Jewish tradition, sections of the Torah (Genesis—Deuteronomy) are read each week in worship. Selections are assigned in order to read through the entire Torah every year. On the day Deuteronomy is completed and Genesis is begun again, there is a great celebration, called Simchat Torah. The scroll of the Torah is paraded through the congregation and there are special prayers and music.

Contributed by Nancy Fisher, Rolling Hills Covenant Church, Torrance, CA

GIRLS' NIGHT OUT

Plan a special candlelight dinner or old-fashioned tea for the girls in your class.

Contributed by Jennifer Tebbutt, Alliance Bible Church, Hillsboro, OR

PARTY FOR THE PASTOR

On or around the pastor's birthday, plan a party honoring the pastor. Students might choose to arrange to wear clothes in the pastor's favorite color, make gifts and cards to present, memorize and recite pastor's favorite Bible passage, and/or serve refreshments. Students may also wish to present skits or write songs about their favorite memories of the pastor.

KID-DECORATED ROOM

Students select a theme for room decoration, then create decorations and/or bring items from home to decorate the room in that way. Every three to six months re-do the decorating.

Theme ideas:

Bible times palace or city, Lakeside, At the Beach, Missionary Travel Agency, Back to the Fifties, On Safari, etc.

GROUP DRAWING

In teams of two or three, students agree on one thing they would like to have in their ideal Sunday School classroom and write it on paper, then pass their papers to the group on their right. Without talking to other teams, each team draws the idea written on the paper it was given. After a few minutes, discuss the drawings. If possible, try to implement some of their changes into your room.

RITE OF PASSAGE

Acknowledge students' accomplishments and progressive maturity by holding a special "graduation" ceremony or meal just before students are promoted to the Junior High class. Involve kids in the planning and execution of this event, making it as formal or informal as resources and preferences dictate. Let kids invite their families and other important people in their lives.

UN-BIRTHDAY PARTY

Hold a class birthday party to celebrate everyone's birthday at one time. Have games, prizes, and traditional birthday party refreshments.

Tips:

1. Plan a gift exchange with each student secretly selecting the name of another student in the class for whom to bring a birthday gift.
2. Talk about what it means to have a "spiritual birthday" (the day a student decides to become a member of God's family). Discuss what it means to become a member of God's family.

Contributed by Nancy Fisher, Rolling Hills Covenant Church, Torrance, CA

VACATION BIBLE SCHOOL HELPERS

Involve fifth and sixth graders as leaders for Vacation Bible School activities. Hold a special training session just for them. During the training, review the Bible stories to be covered. Make the crafts together, demonstrating how students can help younger children as they make their crafts. (Teach students HOW to help others; don't assume they know.) Also, familiarize students with the Vacation Bible School songs. Worksheets for fifth- and sixth-grade levels may be sent home for students to do as homework. This is a big commitment for students, but many of them are ready for it.

Contributed by Vicki Wiley, Cornerstone Bible Church, Glendora, CA

WANT TO JOIN?

Kids love to belong to clubs. Have your class create a name, elect officers and make rules for their Sunday School club. Students may decorate their classroom or make club buttons to wear ("Make Your Own" pin-on buttons may be purchased at craft supply store.).

Variation:

Students meet at someone's home one or two times a month to discuss plans for their club. On Sunday, these plans are discussed and voted on by any students who could not attend the meeting.

BIG BROTHER/ SISTER

Pair students in your class with older Junior High students or even High School students. Use extra time for writing notes or praying for the Big Brothers and Sisters. Invite the older students to spend time with your class one Sunday or during a special event.

Contributed by Brad and Jennifer Tebbutt, Alliance Bible Church, Hillsboro, OR

SECRET SISTERS

For a girls' class, use some extra time to develop "secret sisters" relationships for prayer, encouragement, or even small gifts.

Contributed by Jennifer Tebbutt, Alliance Bible Church, Hillsboro, OR

KEEP 'EM AWAKE

When students lack energetic participation, toss wrapped candies to students who participate by answering a question or contributing to the discussion.

Tip:

Small crackers could also be used.

Contributed by Deborah Barber, Central Church, Memphis, TN

PREDICTIONS

Draw a giant balloon on a large sheet of butcher paper; display in the classroom. Each week, students put stickers on the balloon for attendance, bringing their Bibles, memorizing Bible passages, and bringing a friend. At the beginning of the quarter, students predict how many stickers they will be able to get on the balloon. Write the number somewhere on the balloon. If students meet or beat the number, reward them with a special activity or party.

HOW MANY COOKIES IN THE COOKIE JAR?

To motivate good attendance, set a large, clear cookie jar near the door of the classroom. Each week, as a student arrives, put a cookie in the cookie jar. On an unannounced day, divide the cookies among students who are in attendance.

Tips:

1. Add additional cookies for each student reading weekly Bible devotions or memorizing Bible passages.
2. Use coins instead of cookies. Each quarter, (or at the end of the year), students decide on a way to spend the money that is collected.

THE POINT SYSTEM

Assign a point value for attendance, bringing Bible to Sunday School, memorizing the Bible passage, and completing activities (both in class and weekly devotional). Keep track of points students earn. Provide prizes, parties or privileges that students can earn with a set number of points.

Tips:

1. Prizes could include pencils, small candy bars, fancy erasers, inexpensive toys, books, etc. Parties can include a donut party, pizza party, ice cream party, picnic, game night at teacher's home, movie night, or a trip to a baseball game or amusement park. Privileges might include leading prayer time, selecting a song for praise time, etc.
2. Divide class into teams. Teams compete with each other to earn the most amount of points.
3. Keep track of the points each student has earned on a class chart. Or use game money or slips of paper with point values on them. Provide students with envelopes to keep their "earnings" in.

Contributed by Nancy Land, Branch Fellowship Church, Harleysville, PA; and Deborah Barber, Central Church, Memphis, TN

A CIRCLE OF HANDS BULLETIN BOARD

To emphasize a service theme, have students trace around their hands on construction paper, cut out hand shapes, and mount them on bulletin board. Outline each hand with a silver or gold pen (available at craft stores). Students write their names on their hand shapes and may write or draw ways they use their hand to serve. (Variation: For a Christmas bulletin board, students make hand cut-outs from red and green construction paper and mount them in the shape of a wreath. Attach large bow to top of wreath.)

OUR FAMILY TREE BULLETIN BOARD

Help students celebrate their differences. Bring in leaves from one tree, one leaf for each student. Students trace around their leaves and cut them out. Then students see if they can match leaves exactly. Discuss how, just as leaves from the same tree are all different, so all members of God's family are different. Students meet in groups to find one thing about themselves that is different from everyone else in the group and write it on their leaf. Cut a tree trunk shape from brown paper and mount it on the bulletin board. Students attach their leaves to the tree.

PUZZLE BULLETIN BOARD

To make a graphic display of how all the "pieces" of your class fit together to make a team, letter "Now you are the body of Christ, and each one of you is a part of it" (1 Corinthians 12:27) on a large sheet of paper and attach it to the bulletin board. Cut large puzzle pieces from a sheet of cardboard or foam core. Students write their names on the puzzle pieces, decorate them and glue them around the verse. Optional: Students color the puzzle pieces, write poems or short stories on them, or glue on art materials. (*Variation:* Purchase a puzzle with large puzzle pieces. Students write their names on the backsides of the pieces.)

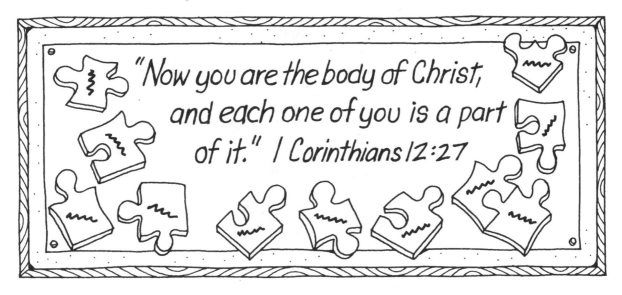

FOLLOWING JESUS BULLETIN BOARD

Mount the heading, "Following Jesus" on the bulletin board. Students trace around their shoes on colored construction paper and cut out shoe shapes, then write the words of the Bible Memory Passage on the footprints, one word on each shape. Cut a path from crumpled brown paper bags or wrapping paper. Mount the path and footprints on bulletin board.

THANK-YOU QUILT BULLETIN BOARD

As a reminder of the good things God gives, make a thank-you quilt bulletin board. On a square of paper or fabric, each student draws or writes about something for which he or she is grateful. Students may border squares with colorful wrapping paper or fabric. Mount squares on bulletin board like a quilt. Label board, "Thank You, God, for What You Have Given Us." **Tip:** Provide a variety of art supplies and decorations (felt scraps, sequins, ribbon, pom-poms, etc.).

WE'RE LOOKING AT GOD'S WORD BULLETIN BOARD

Under the heading, "We're Looking at God's Word," draw a large Bible in the center of the board. To make glasses, students cut apart plastic carriers from soft-drink six-packs (see sketch), then attach chenille wires to each side of plastic rim for ear pieces. Cut noses, mustaches, eyebrows or decorative rims from paper, fake fur, or cloth. Decorate with sequins and collage materials. Mount glasses on bulletin board. Students may draw eyes behind glasses, if desired.

WORKING TOGETHER BULLETIN BOARD

Create a bulletin board that celebrates students' abilities and ways they work together in the body of Christ. Letter "Working Together as Part of God's Family" on bulletin board. Each student cuts out a gear shape from colored construction paper, writes his or her name at the top and a way he or she can serve God by using one special ability. (See sketch.) Mount gear shapes on bulletin board in an interlocking pattern. Discuss how each person is an important part of God's family. **Tip:** Instead of abilities, students may write special facts about themselves or prayer requests on gear shapes. Students may also paste pictures of themselves on the gear shapes.

ALL ABOUT US BULLETIN BOARD

Divide bulletin board or wall space into squares using yarn, one space for each student. (Optional: Place a picture of each student in one corner of his or her space.) Students bring in items that tell about themselves and mount items in their spaces. (For example, a student who enjoys baseball might bring in a picture of a baseball glove.) Students may change decorations each month. If there is not enough space for every student to put up something, feature a few different students each month.

CLASS COMMENTS BULLETIN BOARD

To promote dialogue within your group, try this participative bulletin board. Copy the pattern below. Cover sheets of construction paper with clear Con-Tact® paper (or use cardstock paper). Students trace pattern onto construction paper and cut along indicated lines. Attach to bulletin board with conversation balloons containing students' names and an alliterative word for some form of communication. (Examples: Anita Answers, Gus Gabs, Monica Muses, Susie Says, Ines Implies, Tom Tells, etc.). Label bulletin board, "Class Comments." Each week, put up a question that requires students' opinions. Students write answers on index cards and slip cards under hands, feet and nose of their persons.

Looking for some special ideas to spice up your holiday celebrations at the church? The following are ideas for activities, object lessons, crafts and games that can be used at holiday times.

HOLIDAY SNACK

Use cookie cutters to make Rice Krispies Treats in colors and shapes appropriate to the holiday.

Contributed by Jennifer Tebbutt, Alliance Bible Church, Hillsboro, OR

CREATE-A-STORY CIRCLE

Compose a contemporary story around the theme of the holiday you are observing. Have each student add a line to the story as you go around the circle.

Contributed by Brad and Jennifer Tebbutt, Alliance Bible Church, Hillsboro, OR

HOLIDAY CARDS

Create holiday-themed encouragement cards for absent students, family members, pastoral staff, missionaries, missionaries' kids, etc.

Contributed by Brad Tebbutt, Alliance Bible Church, Hillsboro, OR

DECORATIONS

Decorate the church with banners and/or posters reflecting the holiday theme.

Contributed by Brad and Jennifer Tebbutt, Alliance Bible Church, Hillsboro, OR

FAMILY ACTIVITY BOOKLET

Prepare a family activity booklet at Christmas, Easter and Thanksgiving. Include a calendar with a list of ideas of things students can do each evening such as popping popcorn, watching a related video or reading a story.

Contributed by Sharon McKee, Foothills Bible Church, Littleton, CO

FAR-OUT MENUS

Plan fun Thanksgiving dinner menus for different families or groups. Groups write out or draw menus that include an appetizer, salad, entree, dessert and beverage. Examples of groups to make a meal for: a family stranded on a boat, a family on a deserted island, a family lost in the desert, a group of toddlers.

PIN THE FEATHER ON THE TURKEY

Blindfolded players try to pin tail feathers on the turkey. Draw a large turkey on paper and attach it to the wall. Cut out large turkey tail feathers from construction paper, one for each student. Students may draw pictures of things for which they are thankful for on the feathers. Then kids take turns wearing the blindfold and attaching feathers to turkey.

FEAST OF THE TABERNACLES

Set up a learning center-style celebration to teach about ways people have thanked God throughout history. Because the Feast of Tabernacles was celebrated in autumn around harvest time, it makes a natural celebration at Thanksgiving time. Set up several rooms as Bible-times booths (or tabernacles) by draping material across the ceilings to resemble tents, and put rugs or carpet squares on the floor.

In one booth, have a storyteller telling about the different religious celebrations that have been held throughout history to thank God for the good things He has provided. In other booths, have crafts for students to complete. In one room, serve Bible times or Native American refreshments. (Put a hot air popcorn popper in the middle of the room. Leave the top off, and let the fun fly!)

Contributed by Beth Gresham, Crystal Cathedral, Garden Grove, CA

THANKSGIVING PLAYS

Students perform Bible-times and contemporary skits that show God providing for His people then and now. Select a Thanksgiving Day play for students to perform, or have students write a play themselves. Also select a play that tells a Bible story about how God provided for His people (for example, Moses and the Israelites escaping from Egypt.) Students practice and perform both plays, then discuss how God provided for the characters in each play and how God provides for us today.

Contributed by Beth Gresham, Crystal Cathedral, Garden Grove, CA

POP-UP PLACE CARDS

Students make theme-related pop-up place cards to use during holiday meals.

Contributed by Sharon McKee, Foothills Bible Church, Littleton, CO

INTERGENERATIONAL ADVENT WORKSHOP

On the first Sunday of Advent, families gather for shared supper, worship service and crafts. Crafts may include making an Advent candle wreath, an Advent calendar or symbols from Christmas tree ornaments.

Contributed by Julie Sommers, First Presbyterian Church, Santa Barbara, CA

CHRISTMAS COMMERCIALS

Students create TV commercials incorporating Bible passages and Christmas ornaments. Based on assigned passages of the Christmas story, commercials may incorporate Christmas ornaments, carols and TV jingles. Provide ornaments, songbooks, cassettes and cassette player. Teams present their skits to the class. Optional: Videotape commercials to show at a party.

EDIBLE NATIVITY

Make edible nativity scenes. On a base of foil-covered cardboard, spread prepared frosting, then use graham crackers or pretzel sticks to form sides of stable and manger. People and animals may be made from miniature marshmallows connected by toothpicks, stick pretzels, and animal crackers. Crumble shredded wheat biscuits to create hay. Use other food decorations (dry cereal, chocolate stars, candy sprinkles, etc.) to decorate the nativity scene.

MARSHMALLOW SNOWFLAKES

Make snowflakes by connecting regular and miniature marshmallows with toothpicks and bamboo skewers.

BERRY BASKET SNOWFLAKES

Make snowflakes by cutting shapes from the bottoms of plastic berry or tomato baskets. Glue shapes together with a hot glue gun. Spray with white or silver spray paint; sprinkle glitter on wet paint. Let dry, then hang with yarn.

CHRISTMAS STRING ANGELS

Make economical angel ornaments from scrap materials. Dip heavy string in diluted glue, then evenly wind the string around a plastic soda or detergent bottle top to form angel body (see sketch a). Sprinkle glitter over body.

Next, lay glue-soaked string on wax paper in a double wing shape, and fill in outline with coiled designs (see sketch b). Sprinkle glitter over wings.

After drying overnight, glue wings to back of angel. Glue a round, gold Christmas ornament to top of body for a head. Shape chenille wire or tinsel into a halo, and glue on angel's head. (See sketch c.)

Contributed by Kathleen McIntosh, Vineyard Church, Santa Barbara, CA

a.

b.

c.

BETHLEHEM WALK

Set up your area as a walk through Bethlehem with different Bible-times crafts people. Students move from area to area, learning about life in Bible times as they imagine what Mary and Joseph saw in Bethlehem as they searched for a place to stay.

Suggested activities for each area:

1. *Scribe:* Spread melted wax on cardboard tablets. Students use pencils or cuticle sticks to write on the wax tablets.

2. *Potter:* Provide clay for students to make clay lamps or bowls.

3. *Weaver:* Students weave small mats from paper or yarn.

4. *Baker:* Students make matzo bread.

5. *Carpenter:* Allow students to experiment with planing, chiseling and sawing wood, pounding nail with mallet and making holes with awl or drill.

Contributed by Beth Gresham, Crystal Cathedral, Garden Grove, CA

CHILDREN'S CHRISTMAS MUSICAL

Third- through fifth-grade participants in the second-hour service may become involved with the production of a children's Christmas musical. Kids choose whether they want to be performers or stagehands. Performers make up the choir and actors; stagehands do all the support work: costumes, props, invitations, programs, refreshments, ushers, etc. All kids are honored at the performance.

Contributed by Pam Theis, Northwest Hills Baptist Church, Corvallis, OR

TREE DECORATING

Students make Christmas ornaments, then decorate a Christmas tree to display in some part of the church building. Ornaments may be symbols that tell about Jesus or characters from the Christmas story. Also provide lights, garlands and bows.

Contributed by Beth Gresham, Crystal Cathedral, Garden Grove, CA

HOLIDAY SERVICE PROJECT

Kids plan and supervise a Christmas party for a younger class. The plan might include food (JELL-O Jigglers or Rice Krispies Treats in red and green colors, cut with Christmas cookie cutters), a Christmas craft, a skit or puppet show, and games.

Contributed by Brad and Jennifer Tebbutt, Alliance Bible Church, Hillsboro, OR

HANUKKAH SERVICE

Hold a Hanukkah celebration to introduce kids to the historical meaning of the holiday and help them discover the significance these events can have for contemporary Christians. The celebration may include crafts (dreidels and menorah), special foods, a special candle-lighting service, and a Bible story.

Contributed by Pam Theis, Northwest Hills Baptist Church, Corvallis, OR

NEW YEAR'S PARTY CRACKERS

Make crackers to wish recipients a happy new year. Students write Bible verses and New Year's greetings on slips of paper, and put them inside cardboard toilet paper tubes. Fill the tubes with confetti, wrapped candy, trinkets, and/or little gifts. Wrap the tubes with gift wrap or festive tissue paper; tie the ends with ribbon. Clip the paper at ends to make frills. Decorate with markers, glitter and colorful stickers.

VALENTINE CRAFT

Make heart-themed crafts for Valentine's Day crafts. Use leather strips and heart-shaped pony beads to make key chains, bracelets or bookmarks.

Contributed by Brad and Jennifer Tebbutt, Alliance Bible Church, Hillsboro, OR

VALENTINE JEOPARDY

Set up a Valentine Jeopardy game in which questions review things learned in previous lessons and the prizes are chocolate Kisses. Attach red construction paper squares to a white sheet for the Jeopardy game board. Put answers on transparencies, then at the appropriate time, show them on the overhead.

Game Rules:

Under each category is a point value (100, 200, etc.). Answers to questions for each category are written with an increasing level of difficulty according to the point value. There will be one answer per category, per point value. Contestants select a category and point value. The answer for that spot is read aloud. The first contestant to ring a bell is allowed to give a question to fit that answer. The contestant's response must be phrased in the form of a question. If the contestant is right, he or she is awarded that number of points. If the contestant is not right, one of the other contestants may answer correctly to win the points. A time limit is set for each round. The player with the most points at the end of the round is the winner.

Contributed by Beth Gresham, Crystal Cathedral, Anaheim, CA

PATRICK'S PRESSURE

Before students arrive, hide several green objects (clothing, wrapped candy, toys, etc.) somewhere in the classroom. After students arrive, tell only one of the students, "Patrick," where you hid the objects. Divide the rest of the group into two teams. Have the teams race to find the objects. Teams try to persuade "Patrick" to tell them where the objects are (no body contact allowed!). "Patrick" gives clues to the teams. Whichever team finds the most objects first wins. Read 1 Corinthians 15:33 and discuss peer pressure.

EGG CRATE HOLY WEEK

Fill plastic eggs with small symbols and Scripture references for things Jesus did during Holy Week (the time from Palm Sunday to Easter). Put plastic eggs in an egg carton. As students open eggs, read Scriptures and place symbols on a large map of Jerusalem and the surrounding area to show where each event took place.

Contributed by Nancy Fisher, Rolling Hills Covenant Church, Torrance, CA

EASTER OBJECT LESSON

Teach the Easter story in "the tomb." Turn off the lights, put tables together, cover with blankets, and conduct your class "in the tomb." Compare the darkness of the tomb with the darkness of our lives without Christ; compare the light of day as you leave the tomb with the gift of light that God gave in Jesus.

Contributed by Rob Goff, Alliance Bible Church, Hillsboro, OR

EASTER TREES

Following an Easter egg hunt in which kids find eggs with symbols of the Easter story inside (i.e., thorn, nail, coin, sponge, bread, etc.), groups decorate small, white trees with these items as they tell the Easter story.

We take a picture of each group decorating its tree and slip the photo inside an Easter card, along with an explanation of the significance of each item on the tree. These cards are signed by the students, then addressed to a shut-in or person in need of encouragement. The small group leader (sometimes with students) delivers the tree. It has become a tradition at our church—people love receiving these meaningful trees.

Contributed by Pam Theis, Northwest Hills Baptist Church, Corvallis, OR

EGG HUNT PUZZLE

Take photos of spots around the church. Cut photos into puzzle pieces. Put each puzzle picture in a separate envelope. Hide eggs in locations illustrated in photos. (Some eggs may contain symbols of Holy Week events and some contain treats.)

Divide class into teams. Each team is given one or more envelopes containing the photo puzzle pieces. At a given signal, teams put puzzles together, then retrieve their eggs. The first team to find all their eggs gets a prize. Use symbols in eggs to help tell the story of Holy Week.

Contributed by Nancy Fisher, Rolling Hills Covenant Church, Torrance, CA

DiG iT

Stuff small clay pots with scrolls containing Bible references for Old Testament prophecies about Jesus' birth and life. Or, with a permanent black marker, write references on pot shards. Bury pots or shards in a playground sandbox or a section of soft soil. Or hide them around the classroom. Groups of students search for the pottery, then return to classroom with pots or shards to look up the passages and discuss how Jesus fulfilled those prophecies. Groups report what they have discovered to the whole class.

Contributed by Nancy Fisher, Rolling Hills Covenant Church, Torrance, CA

CHURCH FAMILY WORSHIP SERVICE

Plan an intergenerational worship service on special days such as Father's Day or Mother's Day. For churches where the children have activities they can participate in both hours, bridge the gap between the "Children's Church crowd" and the "Family Worship folks" by providing periodic family worship of a high quality. This kind of service can convey the true experience of community, and can help children to see worship as attractive, understandable, and fun.

Features might include: coloring activities to work on in one's seat, an intergenerational worship team, special numbers in music by children and youth, a sermon as a fun object lesson, a responsive reading which underscores the main thrust ("The Church is God's family, He wants us to be devoted to one another."), interactive learning experiences, and banners which remain up after the service as reminders of what was learned.

Contributed by Pam Theis, Northwest Hills Baptist Church, Corvallis, OR

SPECIAL GUEST DAY

Let kids invite guests to participate in class activities on special days. Prior to holidays such as Mother's, Father's and Grandparents' Days, have kids invite special adults to come to class with them. Plan a modified lesson with learning center-type activities that kids and guests may rotate through at their own pace. Activities might include a silly hat photo center (kids and guests choose hats to wear, and pose for an instant photo), a mixer requiring peoples' initials next to little-known facts ("Someone whose dad is a fireman." "Someone who has been to Hawaii."), a cooperative art project and a game table. Post instructions by each center, and spend your time helping kids and guests have a good time together.

Tip:

If the concept of "special guest" is communicated appropriately, kids without the requisite parent will not be made to feel uncomfortable. For example, say, "Father's Day is a good day to think about all the people who are special to us. Think about who you'd like to invite to our party. Maybe you have a grandparent, or an uncle or older brother who has been kind of like a dad to you." And if someone wants to bring grandma on Father's Day, welcome her, too!

Contributed by Lynnette Pennings, Faith Lutheran Church, Carpinteria, CA

MISSIONS & SERVICE PROJECTS

These ideas will help you teach your students about the missionary involvement of your church, denomination or private missions groups.

ADOPT A MISSIONARY KID

If your church sponsors missionaries with children near the ages of your class, you can "adopt" the missionary's kid by becoming pen pals. Kids can take turns writing to the child, or the entire class can participate in group projects like exchanging audio cassettes, video cassettes, faxes or E-mail.

CARD MINISTRY

Students make cards using rubber stamps, markers, and/or tissue paper on construction paper. Check with your church office or pastor for a list of people who might appreciate receiving special greetings. (Examples: Illness or death in the family, new baby, wedding.) Students create appropriate cards and send them.

FIVE-MINUTE MISSIONS

Spend five minutes of each class discussing a different missionary. Help students find his or her country on a globe. Read excerpts from a missions brochure or newsletter about the missionary. Discuss any needs the missionary has or special challenges the missionary faces. Guide students to make prayer request suggestions for the missionary you discussed.
Contributed by Nancy Land, Branch Fellowship Church, Harleysville, PA

COMIC BOOKS

Students work individually or with partners to make comic strips with advice for younger children on how to obey God's commands. Comic strips should have at least five frames. Completed comic strips are collected and stapled together, forming one or more books to be given to a younger class.
Contributed by Jessie Schut, Covenant Christian Reformed Church, Edmonton, AB

DEVELOPING STEWARDSHIP

Distribute wallets containing a dollar each. Students plan and carry out a way to make the money grow. (Example: Students pool money to buy baking supplies and hold a bake sale.) Students then donate the money earned to a missions project or a local charity.
Contributed by Nancy Fisher, Rolling Hills Covenant Church, Torrance, CA

MISSION FAIRE

Set up tables around the room and decorate each to represent a different continent. Establish a theme for each continent/table. (Examples: True Life Missionary Stories. Scripture Research. Prayers for Unreached People.) Have a leader at each table to explain the theme and encourage discussion.

Create a passport that kids will have stamped as they visit each continent. Break class into groups with each group spending ten minutes in each continent. At each table, groups complete an activity or discussion, receive a snack and souvenir typical of that continent and have their passports stamped.

FOOD SCAVENGER HUNT

Divide class into teams. Each team receives a sheet listing food items and point values. During the week, students ask neighbors and friends for food donations. The following week, teams bring food items and calculate their points. Prizes are given to the winning team. Food is then delivered to a local community food distribution project.

Contributed by Nancy Fisher, Rolling Hills Covenant Church, Torrance, CA

HOLIDAY BASKETS

Prepare special holiday goody baskets for children or adults with diabetes. Students bake low sugar cookies, then pack cookies in baskets along with low-sugar recipes, fruit, sugar-free candy and notes of encouragement. Deliver baskets.

Contributed by Deborah Barber, Central Church, Memphis, TN

ALL-CHURCH LITANY

In groups, write a special prayer or litany to be used during the service by the entire congregation. Practice the litany together, and allow the class or group to lead the congregation in prayer.

KIDS' SACKS

Make simple burlap sacks to fill with hygiene items or gifts for children at a local shelter. Students use acrylic or fabric paint to decorate sacks, then fill sacks with collected items (toothbrush and paste, comb, soap, or crayons, markers, puzzle books, etc.). Tie bags closed with yarn or twine and attach notes telling about the givers or sharing God's love. Deliver bags to a local shelter.

Contributed by Nancy Fisher, Rolling Hills Covenant Church, Torrance, CA

MISSIONARY BIOGRAPHIES

Great books can spark kids' interest in missions. Look for collections of short missionary biographies for browsing in a missions corner of your classroom. Or for a service project, have students take turns reading portions into a cassette recorder. The tapes can be placed in your church library for use by sight-disabled people.

MISSIONS TALK SHOW

Arrange for a missionary or a representative of a local missions organization to come and talk with students in a "talk show" format. Before the visitor arrives, kids think of questions for the guest. Get a "ham" to play the role of talk show host, and have fun interviewing your guest.

THANK-YOU LETTERS

As a group, students write thank-you letters acknowledging the efforts of people who help make your community a safer place. Send thank-you letters directly to the people being thanked; or send letters to the editor of the local newspaper for publication.

Contributed by Jessie Schut, Covenant Christian Reformed Church, Edmonton, AB

NURSING HOME TRIP

On the Sunday closest to Christmas, we load the students up on a bus and go to sing our Christmas songs at a nursing home. We let the kids know what to expect and how to minister. For several Sundays prior to the visit, kids make cards to give out. (This facilitates interaction.)

The students have a great experience, teachers get a break from preparing a Sunday School lesson, and we don't have to worry about substitutes for all the teachers who are out of town, as this trip takes less adult supervision than a normal Sunday School morning.

Contributed by Pam Theis, Northwest Hills Baptist Church, Corvallis, OR

VIDEO POST CARD

Instead of written greetings to missionaries, shut-ins, or sick classmates, arrange for someone to come into class for the last ten or fifteen minutes of a session and tape greetings from the kids.

Contributed by Brad Tebbutt, Alliance Bible Church, Hillsboro, OR

WRITE IT OUT!

As a class, write a letter to the editor suggesting possible solutions for a community, national or worldwide problem.

Contributed by Nancy Fisher, Rolling Hills Covenant Church, Torrance, CA

CHILDREN'S CARNIVAL

Students plan and put on a carnival for children in a preschool day care program. Each group of three or four students selects and leads an activity such as facepainting, fishing for candy or a preschool game. Also, students may entertain preschoolers by singing songs or performing skits.

Contributed by Deborah Barber, Central Church, Memphis, TN

ONE MILE OF CANS

Help kids initiate and kick off a community campaign to collect enough cans of food to stretch one mile (approximately 15,840 2-lb. cans). Donate cans to a local food distribution charity.

HAT AUCTION

Purchase inexpensive straw hats. Provide students with glue, ribbons, fabric, flowers, fake fruit and other craft items. Students decorate hats, then hold an auction to sell hats. Money raised from auction is then donated to a charity of the students' choice.

SHELTER MEAL

Kids plan a menu, shop for food, prepare the food and serve it at a local mission or shelter.

PRESCHOOL CHRISTMAS OUTREACH

One Saturday morning in December, we invited all the preschoolers of the community to "Come to the Manger," to hear about and interact with the real meaning of Christmas. The children were received at the door in small groups, each guided by a "Guardian Angel" (one of our youths wearing a shiny garland as a halo). The Guardian Angels directed children through all the activities we had available for them:

Joseph's Carpenter Shop—Kids hammered with wood and nails.

Bethlehem Barnyard—Petting zoo with goat, rabbit, donkey (any animals we could find).

The Best Gift—Kids wrapped a heart with a picture of Jesus in it inside a box. We provided boxes, paper, bows, and tape.

Bethlehem's Babies—Dolls, diapers, cribs, strollers, blankets, bottles, etc. Children played with babies amid guided conversation.

Cuddle Baby Jesus—Children each made a darling "baby Jesus" out of soft heads and blankets. Each got to keep one.

Come to the Master—We built a manger scene with painted backdrop. Each child came, put his or her Baby Jesus in the manger, and had a picture taken. (This is better than a picture with Santa Claus any day!)

Cookie Decorating—Kids decorated and ate sugar cookies.

Make a Star—A glue and glitter experience.

Candy Cane Witness—Kids made bead candy canes on pipe cleaners and received a card telling the origin of candy canes.

Make a Nativity—Kids assembled a paper nativity scene.

All centers included guided conversation. After these experiences, we all met in the sanctuary where the older students acted out the Christmas story and we sang Christmas carols.

Contributed by Cindy Taylor, Northwest Hills Baptist Church, Corvallis, OR

LEARNING ACTIVITIES

Some of these ideas are for specific stories, others are for ongoing projects. Some will help you introduce a Bible story or lesson focus, others will help you review the Bible story or lesson focus. All of these ideas are innovative ways to review the lesson, Bible story and/or the lesson focus.

WHAT'S MY LINE?

Here's a biblical twist on the old radio and TV show. A teacher or guest dresses up as a Bible character whose identity is revealed through questions from competing teams. Divide class into teams. Each team selects a representative and suggests questions for the representative to ask. Representatives for each team ask questions that must be answered with "yes," "no" or "maybe." Representatives return to their teams; teams decide who the Bible character is and write out their guesses. Finally, the Bible character reveals his or her identity. A prize may be given to each team that guessed correctly.

Contributed by Beth Gresham, Crystal Cathedral, Anaheim, CA

ARMOR OF GOD

Paint a life-size Roman soldier in full armor on wood or heavy cardboard. Cut out a hole for a real head. Take photos of students with their heads poking through hole. Discuss how each piece of armor was critical to a Roman soldier. Read Ephesians 6:11-17 and discuss how Paul labeled each piece of armor. Display pictures in classroom.

Contributed by Nancy Fisher, Rolling Hills Covenant Church, Torrance, CA

BILLBOARD CONTEST

Groups of students design billboards with slogans that communicate the message of the day. Each group presents its billboard to the class to be judged by applause. Billboard with the loudest applause wins the contest. Display billboards in a hallway or common area.

MULTIMEDIA STORIES

With some help from you, Bible story videos can be an excellent way to make Bible stories come alive. Before showing the video, review the Bible's account of the story to be seen. When the movie is over, review what students saw, asking several questions to help students compare the actual Bible story with the video's representation of it. **How is this movie just like the story in the Bible? How is it different? What parts have been added by the movie maker's imagination? How would you have told this part of the story differently?**

Contributed by Nancy Land, Branch Fellowship Church, Harleysville, PA

CURRENT COMICS

Collect comic strips from local papers, covering up the conversation in the speech balloons. Students fill in their own conversation ideas based on the lesson focus of the day.

ROUND-ROBIN STORIES

Each student writes the beginning of a story that illustrates the day's lesson. After a minute or two, say, "Change." Students pass their papers to the right, quickly read what's written there, then continue writing the story. Students continue to change papers and write until they receive their own papers back. Give students one minute to write conclusions for their stories. Then let volunteers read stories aloud.

REVIEW WALK

This simple technique for review gets kids moving and encourages response from the silent types. Number separate sheets of paper, one for each student, and place papers in a circle on the floor. Number corresponding slips of paper and place in a paper bag. Play music on a cassette or recite a Bible passage while students walk around outside of circle. When music or passage ends, students stand on papers. Select a number from bag. The student standing on the corresponding sheet of paper answers a question about the lesson. *Variation:* Write the names of Bible characters or books of the Bible on papers. Then write clues for each character or book on slips of paper. Play game as above. When music stops, pull a slip from bag and read the clue. The student standing on the corresponding paper gets one point (or a prize).

MEDIA MESSAGES

Show magazine advertisements that advise people to live a certain way and discuss the messages being conveyed. Compare the messages from advertisements with messages from the Bible. Students create their own advertisements based on ways the Bible says to live.

QUICK POEMS

Select a theme word that sums up the lesson's focus. Students suggest words that rhyme with the theme word. Write on chalkboard or large sheet of paper. Students then write short, four-line poems about the lesson theme, using the suggested words.

CLUE GAME

Play a game of logical deduction to reinforce life application of the day's Bible truth. Divide class into at least three teams. Make a list of 14 names of kids (WHO?), 14 places kids might go (WHERE?) and 14 activities kids might do (WHAT?). Each team copies the list. Write each item from the list on a separate index card. Sort index cards by category. Choose one card from each group without looking and place the selected cards in an envelope. Shuffle and distribute remaining index cards equally among teams.

The goal of the game is to discover WHO (witnessed about Christ) WHERE, doing WHAT. Teams take turns guessing to help determine which cards are hidden in the envelope. Guesses must be phrased, "I think (John) witnessed about Christ in the (park) while (hiking)." After a team has stated its guess, the other teams are asked if they can disprove the guess. (For example, Team 3 might be holding the bus card, so they would say, "It wasn't done on the bus.") Continue play with each team taking a turn until one team is able to say which cards are in the envelope. Open the envelope to confirm the answer.

Tips:

1. This activity provides an opportunity to discuss how the kids might show or talk about God's love under similar circumstances.
2. By changing the phrasing, other life application situations can be discussed. Examples: "(Joey) show God's love at (the swimming pool) by (sharing his cookies)." "(Karen) showed God's forgiveness (on the playground) while (playing tether ball)."

Contributed by Nancy Fisher, Rolling Hills Covenant Church, Torrance, CA

STORY QUILT

Using fabric paints, students draw or trace pictures showing different parts of a Bible story onto separate quilt squares. Sew squares together, using fabric borders in between. Complete quilt with stuffing and backing. Use yarn ties along seams and at corners to hold quilt together. (See sketch.) Raffle quilt as a fundraiser or give it as a gift to a special member of the church.

Contributed by Theresa Grossklaus, Trinity Lutheran Church, Lewiston, ID

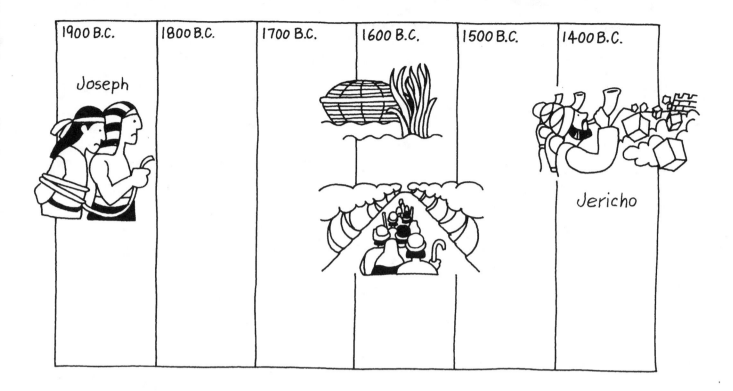

TIME LINE

To help students understand Bible chronology, create a time line to display in the classroom. On butcher paper, draw lines to designate time divisions, labeling dates at the top of each line. (See sketch.) Provide resource books with time-line information. Students draw pictures or cut out Bible story clip art pictures and attach them at the appropriate points along the time line. Or add events throughout the year as they are studied. **Tip:** A time line can also be made along a blank wall by using yarn stretched from ceiling to floor as time markers. Tape or pin labels to the wall in appropriate time slots.

BROWN BAG LESSONS

After telling the Bible story, divide class into groups of two to four students. Give each group a paper bag holding three to five items that relate to the lesson. Groups retell the Bible story using the items in their bags.

Contributed by Nancy Fisher, Rolling Hills Covenant Church, Torrance CA

FOILED BY AN IMPRESSION

Make masks by gently pressing squares of heavy aluminum foil around faces to show shape and features. Punch holes for eyes and mouth, folding over any sharp edges. Decorate masks with sequins, rick-rack, yarn, feathers, etc.

GAME SHOWS

Adapt favorite TV game shows to review lesson material. Some favorites might be: "Wheel of Fortune" with phrases from Bible passages as puzzles, "Family Feud" with names of Bible characters or books of the Bible, and "Name That Tune" using favorite praise songs or hymns and their subject matter.

Contributed by Beth Gresham, Crystal Cathedral, Garden Grove, CA

VIDEO SKITS

If your class has polished a skit, arrange for someone to come to class to film the skit. The video can be shown to other classes in your department or sent to someone special.

Contributed by Brad Tebbutt, Alliance Bible Church, Hillsboro, OR

Have you ever gotten through your whole lesson before class time was up and wondered what you were going to do with your students? Do you sometimes find that your students get restless or lethargic half-way through the lesson? Then these ideas are for you. These activities last from five to ten minutes. For the most part, they can be used without any additional materials. And most of them help you keep teaching while the students have fun.

COFFEE-CAN ICE CREAM

Put the following ingredients in a self-locking bag:

1/2 cup (.12 l) whipping cream,
1 cup (.24 l) milk,
1/4 cup (.6 l) sugar,
1 teaspoon (5 ml) vanilla,
1 egg.

Place sealed bag in a 3-lb. (1.41-l) coffee can filled with ice and salt. Tape can shut and roll around on the floor during the lesson. The ice cream will set in 10-15 minutes.

Contributed by Nancy Fisher, Rolling Hills Covenant Church, Torrance, CA

CHAIR ROTATION

To liven up one class, expand the time, and catch the students' attention, we taught from all four sides of the classroom. At three different times in the morning we asked the kids to rotate their chairs a quarter turn. It really mixed up the back row bunch!

Contributed by Rob Goff, Alliance Bible Church, Hillsboro, OR

MAKING BUTTER

Pour 1 pint (.4 l) heavy cream or whipping cream into a clean, quart-size jar with a tight-fitting lid. Shake the jar and pass it around the group, each student taking a turn at shaking it. When the butter has completely separated from the whey, open the jar, pour off the liquid and spread butter on crackers or bread sticks.

Contributed by Nancy Fisher, Rolling Hills Covenant Church, Torrance, CA

FILL IN

Choose a word or short phrase and draw blanks on a chalkboard or large sheet of paper in place of each letter. As students transition from one activity to another, allow them to guess a letter. When a student is ready to guess the answer, he or she signals to stop the game. If the guess is correct, the game ends. If the answer is incorrect, the game continues.

Contributed by Nancy Fisher, Rolling Hills Covenant Church, Torrance, CA

QUICK DRAW

As a group, list the events that took place in a Bible story. Write each event on a separate slip of paper and put in a paper bag. Students form teams. Each team selects a slip of paper from the paper bag. At your signal, one member from each team races to the chalkboard and starts to draw a picture about the story. At your signal to change, a second team member takes over drawing the picture, and the first player returns to his or her team. Continue to play until each team member has had a chance to add to the drawing. Teams then guess what event other teams have depicted in their drawings.

ADDED-TO GAMES

Have various board games available for use when there is extra time or for students that arrive early. Make additional game cards for games that review past Sunday School lessons.

Contributed by Nancy Land, Branch Fellowship Church, Harleysville, PA

HOW MANY POINTS?

Students answer true-or-false questions about themselves, adding or subtracting points as indicated for each answer. At the end, students add up their points to see who has the highest and lowest numbers.

Suggestions for Questions:

1. If you are wearing black shoes, give yourself 10 points.

2. If you are wearing blue socks, take away 5 points.

3. If you were born on an odd-numbered day of the month (such as 1, 17, or 29), give yourself 25 points.

4. If you were born in a month that ends with a *y*, take away 10 points.

5. If you are under 12 years old, add the amount of your age.

6. If you are wearing shoes that are not black, give yourself 15 points.

7. If you are wearing socks that are not white, take away 5 points.

8. If you have a dog, take away 5 points.

9. If you have a pet that is not a cat, add 15 points.

10. If you are wearing more than one color, add 25 points.

MEDIA WATCH

Collect information on current releases of songs, videos, magazines, etc. and share this information with students during class. You may even wish to include evaluations of wholesome secular materials along with evaluation and promotional information on Christian media.

Contributed by Brad Tebbutt, Alliance Bible Church, Hillsboro, OR

GRAFFITI

Cover a wall with butcher paper or use a large blackboard for your canvas. Write the point of your lesson all over the wall or board. Use colored chalk to creatively print in huge letters a saying or phrase to make your point. Words can crawl all over your board, up and down, diagonally, or in curves.

Contributed by Karen Perkins, Walnut Creek Presbyterian Church, Walnut Creek, CA

TWENTY QUESTIONS

Think of a Bible character or a central object in a Bible story (e.g., the Ark in the story of Noah). Students ask up to twenty questions which can be answered with a "yes" or "no". Student making the correct guess tells part of the story or what can be learned from the story. Then student thinks of a Bible character or an object, and the game continues.

VIDEO PICS

Find some crazy, old movies or TV shows and record three- to five-minute clips that can be shown occasionally as a special feature. Kids really enjoy laughing at some of the older shows.

Contributed by Jennifer Tebbutt, Alliance Bible Church, Hillsboro, OR

IN THE HOT SEAT

Put chairs in a circle. Label one chair the "Hot Seat." At your signal, students exchange seats. The one sitting in the Hot Seat answers a question about the Bible story or recites the Bible passage.

POSITIVE PARENTING FOR THE PRETEEN YEARS

BY TOM PRINZ, M.S., M.F.C.C.

Have you ever met a parent who wouldn't like a little more help in dealing with preteens? Not likely! These articles for parents place a goldmine of great information at your fingertips and provide a valuable link between the classroom and the home.

Written by Tom Prinz, Licensed Educational Psychologist and Marriage, Family and Child Counselor, this series of 24 articles speaks gently and frankly about typical issues confronting the parents of preteens, such as dealing with anger, discipline, and chores. Mail copies of the articles home once each month; use this section of the book as a troubleshooting encyclopedia when you get questions; or use the articles as the basis of a parenting course—but do use them!

ABOUT THE AUTHOR:

Tom Prinz, a Marriage, Family and Child Counselor and a Licensed Educational Psychologist, has been in private practice for over 12 years. Tom counsels with children, teenagers, and adults, specializing in parenting issues and in marriage counseling. Tom has conducted hundreds of seminars on a variety of topics.

Prior to his private practice, Tom worked as a school psychologist for eight years. He graduated from U.C. Berkeley with a master's degree in mechanical engineering and worked for Shell Oil Company for seven years before changing careers, getting a second master's degree in counseling/psychology from Cal State Los Angeles.

Tom and his wife Pam have three young adult children, Robyn, Matthew, and Chrissy. Pam works as a school psychologist. Tom has published two books, *Dragon Slaying for Parents*, and *Dragon Slaying for Couples*.

PARENTS ARE BLAMED, BUT NEVER TRAINED

An insight I began sharing years ago during parent education classes is this: Parents are blamed, but never trained. Parents are often blamed for the mistakes of their children, but very few parents ever receive formal training for the most important role of their lives—helping their children to become responsible, confident adults.

Even sadder, many parents do not realize the need for formal training to enable them to become effective parents. Most parents either do exactly what their parents did, or the complete opposite because they hated what was done to them so much. Parents need to gain parenting strategies or tools that have proven to be effective and positive.

CHANGES IN CULTURE

Many parents today feel overwhelmed by popular culture and more helpless than their parents. Being a successful parent in the 1990s is much more demanding than it was 20 or 30 years ago. The reasons for this are many: through many hours of television viewing, magazines and newspapers, kids are exposed to a violent society with weakening sexual morals; drugs and alcohol are more available today; the divorce rate is higher; more mothers are working outside the home; and society is more mobile, resulting in less support from an extended family.

Children used to look at ministers, teachers, neighbors, and heroes as leaders. Now they look to cartoon super heroes, rap groups, and celebrities pushing sneakers as their role models. It's what makes child raising harder. It's not just that parents have less time to spend with their kids, it's that they have to spend more of that time doing battle with their own culture!

SKILLS AND TOOLS

Most parents look upon the teenage years with a tremendous amount of fear and anxiety, anticipating rebellion. Successful parenting is not a matter of luck; it requires skills and tools, and those can be learned. A key time for parents to begin to refine their parenting strategies is the time immediately preceding the teenage years. Your task as a parent will be much easier and you will feel more confident in your role as you acquire new tools and strategies.

When adults have trouble fixing a car or remodeling a home, they will readily consider upgrading their tools. However, when dealing with preteens, it's easier to blame the kids when things go awry, rather than to look at our own parenting skills.

This is the first in a series of articles offering many helpful and practical strategies to equip you to deal with your kids now and through the teenage years. You will also learn about hidden factors that may interfere with your ability to apply the parenting tools consistently and effectively.

A CHALLENGE TO YOU:

1. What did your parents do that you liked? What did they do that you did not like?

2. What is your attitude about the need for parents to receive training to be effective parents?

3. What can you do to show your openness to new ideas that will make life easier for you and your kids?

LEARN YOUR CHILD'S LANGUAGE OF LOVE

Do you love your child? I'm sure that most of the time you would quickly answer, "Of course!" Nearly all parents truly love their children. However, it has been my experience through 20 years of working with parents, children and teens in seminars and private counseling settings that many youngsters do not feel loved. How can that be? Evidently, loving our kids is not enough. We must show love to them in ways that help them to feel loved.

The love we show to our kids must imitate the love God has shown to us. God loves us no matter what; His love is unconditional. A well-known college football coach was once asked to comment on his son who was a star on his football team. His response was remarkable: "I think that my son has done an outstanding job on this team, but I would be just as proud of him if he had never played the game at all." That is the challenge we all face as parents; how can we demonstrate unconditional love to our kids so they feel loved, no matter what they do?

WAYS TO SHOW LOVE

Three simple ways to show love are through **eye contact, physical contact** and **focused attention.**

When you talk to your child, look at him or her. Our words mean very little if our body lan-

guage does not convey the same message. For instance, if you are reading the newspaper while you ask your kid how her day was, you will probably not get a very positive response. I remember a teenager telling his parents that when they stood at his door and said "good night" to him, it wasn't as special as when they sat down by the side of his bed, at his eye level.

A second way to show love to your child is through physical contact. Some youngsters are more receptive to physical contact than others. Don't give up if your preteen seems unresponsive; use moments when he might be tired or have a headache and give him a back rub. Physical contact does not have to be a big bear hug; giving a kid a "high-five" or simply touching her on the shoulder will register, too. Research shows that teenagers whose parents are warm and affectionate are less likely to use drugs than children whose parents are cold and distant.

A third way to show love to your child is through focused attention. Spending time with a child individually is one of the most effective ways to show love. Examples can include working on a project together, taking a walk, going to the movies, taking a train trip, going shopping, or hundreds of other ideas.

CONVEY A CHILD'S VALUE

Eye contact, physical contact and focused attention, when given in abundance, will help to keep your child's feelings of worth at a high level. When a child feels valued, his or her behavior will be much more positive than if he or

(Continued on next page.)

(Continued from previous page.)

she feels valueless. Sometimes preteens' behavior may be so bad that we feel like ignoring them or sending them to their rooms; but sometimes, sitting down with them, looking at them, talking to them and touching them will result in a much happier evening.

LEARN THE LANGUAGE

Another very important way to show love to your child is to **convey love in his or her language of love.** Once when I was taking my daughter to the show, I asked her what show she wanted to see. Her choice was not appealing to me, and I tried to talk her out of it; but then I realized that if my aim was to show love to her, the love needed to be in her language of love. A teenager I counseled once complained that her father would take her out for pizza, but he wouldn't let her order Canadian bacon and pineapple because he didn't like it. The time and money he spent was not having the impact he had hoped for because he was not showing his daughter love in her language. When you show an interest in your child's language of love, you are being sympathetic to his or her needs.

Many parents have trouble showing love in ways their kids understand because they did not receive love in these same ways from their own parents. We all tend (consciously or subconsciously) to turn our current homes into a replica of the home we came from. Consider the ways in which you received love, and then consider whether you may have to work extra hard to show love in ways your kids understand.

A CHALLENGE TO YOU:

1. Which of the three ways to show love (eye contact, physical contact and focused attention) did you receive as a child? Which did you not receive?

2. Which of the three ways to show love (eye contact, physical contact and focused attention) do you need to display more of? How do you plan to do it?

3. What activities does your child recognize as his or her language of love?

HOW TO ~~TALK~~ LISTEN TO YOUR CHILD

Many parents ask me how they should talk to make their kids listen to them. I tell them the most important thing parents can learn is how to really listen to their kids. If we do not listen to our kids, they will not listen to us. Listening is a skill that can be developed. It is a skill that you may not have observed in your parents when you were a child. Did your parents listen to you as a child, or did you grow up understanding that "children are to be seen and not heard"?

One of my favorite quotes is, "A joy not shared is cut in half, and a sorrow not shared is doubled." If you win a tournament, or an honor or a promotion at work but have no one to share it with, the victory may seem hollow. If you are suffering in pain or disappointment, or become frustrated about a relationship and have no one to share it with, the pain increases.

How sad I felt in a counseling session when a 17-year-old boy told his parents that he had decided not to share his joys or his sorrows with his parents. Fortunately, this family is working on these issues, and hopefully by the time he leaves home he will be able to share his joys and his sorrows with his parents. What drove this youngster to feel uncomfortable sharing his feelings, thoughts and ideas with his parents?

ACCEPT FEELINGS

There are many ways that parents unintentionally inhibit their kids from sharing. One of the most common is a parent's inability to accept the child's feelings. A child says that she is afraid of the dark and the parent responds, "You don't need to be afraid of the dark—our house is safe." A child says, "You love my brother more than me," and the parent responds, "No we don't, we love you both the same." In both situations the parent has not accepted the child's feelings. It's better to say things like, "I know that the house can seem scary at night," or "Boy, I bet that really makes you feel sad to feel we love your brother more than you." Statements like these are sympathetic responses to kids' feelings, responses that validate and affirm their feelings.

Next, gently try to discover what has led to those feelings, and follow up with some reassuring statements. It's important to accept feelings even if the logic the child has used to arrive at those feelings is not sound. Feelings themselves are neither right nor wrong, they are just there.

HOLD THE ADVICE

If a child shares feelings or ideas and automatically receives advice instead of attentive listening, communication will be shut down. Listen carefully, praise the ideas, and ask if your child wants suggestions before offering advice or solutions.

Always telling your son or daughter a better way to do something will not encourage sharing. Saying, "I like the *B* you got on your report card, but if you'd try

(Continued on next page.)

•

(Continued from previous page.)

harder you could get an *A*," will inhibit a kid that might have wanted to express his or her own feelings of disappointment and frustration.

Being critical and sarcastic is another way to stifle communication. A young man in counseling who had to use a crutch due to arthritis in his hip expressed anger to his father for making fun of his limp. Sarcasm is a trait many parents have learned from their parents and may even accept as normal.

Simply not being available will also make it difficult for your child to express him- or herself. Kids typically won't share things if you march into their rooms and say, "Share with me," but they will usually express themselves more readily if you are taking them out to dinner, or to a ball game, or shopping.

iT'S NEVER TOO LATE

Many parents feel guilty that they haven't responded appropriately in the past to their kids' feelings and ideas, but don't let that stop you from changing your ways. Discuss your shortcomings with your child and commit to becoming a better listener. Don't let guilt keep you from doing what's right; and it's never too late to do what's right.

A CHALLENGE TO YOU:

1. During your childhood, did your parents really listen to you? If not, what did they do that kept you from sharing with them?

2. Think about a recent time your child shared his or her feelings and you did not really accept them. Try to discuss those feelings with him or her now.

HELPING YOUR PRETEEN DEAL WITH ANGER

Your kids may get straight *A*s in school or star on athletic teams, but all those accomplishments will be for naught if they do not learn how to express their anger appropriately. Teaching children how to deal with anger is one of the most important responsibilities a parent has.

When our children were approximately 8, 10 and 12, we had a family meeting to discuss how our family was dealing with anger. Part way through our meeting two of our children got up from the table crying and left for their rooms; our other child sat at the table a few more minutes, then got up angry and went to his room. Although the meeting was painful, it definitely illustrated that our family was not doing a very good job of expressing anger in healthy ways! It made us realize that we needed to teach our children how to deal with anger appropriately, and the results of our efforts have been very positive.

It's natural to get upset when a child yells at you or says "I hate you," or hits a sibling in anger. Children are not born with an innate ability to express anger effectively. They must be taught how to express anger in constructive ways. Unfortunately, many parents do not realize the need to teach their kids *how* to express their anger. Many parents have

not had help in learning to express their own anger effectively. When I have asked groups of parents if they were able to express their anger to their own parents, only four or five hands in every 100 go up, illustrating how few parents were taught how to deal with anger in a healthy way.

THE ANGER LADDER

Let's consider the range of ways kids and parents express anger. Imagine a ladder and at the top of the ladder is the most effective way to express anger, and at the bottom of the ladder is the worst way to deal with anger. Imagine yourself as a child, angry at your father because you feel you have too many chores. The steps of the ladder going from best to worst would be as follows:

BEST WAY TO EXPRESS ANGER:

1. Tell Dad you are upset about the chores. The two of you talk calmly to resolve the problem (less chores, more money, more time to complete them, etc.). (Anger is acknowledged and dealt with appropriately in a direct, healthy manner.)

2. Yell at Dad that you are upset about the chores. (Directing anger toward Dad and mentioning the problem, chores, is healthy but yelling is not healthy.)

3. Yelling at Dad, "I hate you." (Directing anger at Dad is healthy, but the yelling and nonspecific "I hate you" is not.)

4. Slamming a door, or breaking something.

5. Hitting a younger sibling. (While the results of points four and five are undesirable, they rank higher up the ladder than six and seven because the anger is at least more observable, and therefore, easier to deal with.)

6. Keeping anger in. (This approach is very destructive because it will usually result in some physical problems, and will often develop into a passive-aggressive way of dealing with anger.)

7. Passive-aggressive approach to dealing with anger. (The passive-aggressive way of dealing with anger is the most destructive because the child is usually

(Continued on next page.)

(Continued from previous page.)

not even aware that he or she is demonstrating anger, and the results can be extremely negative to the child him- or herself. One definition of passive-aggressive behavior is an action that makes someone angry while unconsciously hurting oneself.) Some typical examples are procrastinating, dawdling or moving slowly, getting *D*s and *F*s in school, doing drugs or alcohol, not taking one's medication for Attention Deficit Disorder and having a messy room.

All kids will show some passive-aggressive behaviors. And, to a certain degree, that's OK. For example, your child may keep his or her room looking like a disaster zone. Most parents misinterpret the reason for a messy room and/or feel that they are losing control if they allow their kids to make decisions about how their rooms will look. However, it's often best to allow kids to have messy rooms for at least part of the week, otherwise they may opt for more destructive ways of being passive aggressive, such as getting low grades. Parents of preteens need to pick their battles carefully, concentrating on more important issues and challenges. A messy room can simply be one way for a preteen to be different from his or her parents.

Your child's position on the anger ladder may vary from day to day, but will also be influenced by his or her personality. Some kids come into the world with a tendency to blast you with their anger by yelling at you, while others tend to keep their anger in.

Regardless of a child's natural tendencies in expression, it is very important for parents to create a climate in which kids are able to express their feelings, including anger.

EXPRESS ANGER POSITIVELY

There are several ways to help preteens learn how to express their anger in a more positive manner.

◆ The first is to model appropriate behavior when you express anger to them and to others.

◆ Another way is to encourage kids to tell you what you might have done lately that makes them angry. Then be prepared to simply listen, accept their feelings, and possibly discuss some solutions to the problem.

◆ Some preteens will definitely need to be encouraged to verbalize their anger: Give them permission.

◆ Reward your preteens verbally and/or with tangible rewards when they express anger appropriately.

◆ It will also be necessary at times to enforce a penalty, such as a fine or grounding, when kids express their anger in inappropriate ways (by swearing, hitting, or breaking something.) For less destructive expression, such as slamming a door, it may be appropriate to simply ignore the behavior and make an effort later to encourage kids to express their feelings.

In short, parents can teach their preteens to move toward the top of the anger ladder by frequently asking if they are angry about anything parents have done, ignoring some inappropriate ways of expressing anger, and punishing destructive, inappropriate ways of expressing anger. Parents have the power to negotiate solutions to problems with their kids; kids do not have the power to do that. So if your goal is for your children to express anger appropriately, you'll need to reach compromises with your kids whenever possible. In this way, you are modeling behavior that is considerate and sympathetic of their needs.

A CHALLENGE TO YOU:

1. Reflect on the ways anger was dealt with in your family when you were a teenager.

2. Ask your child if you have done anything lately that makes him or her angry, and discuss a solution to the problem.

3. Discuss the anger ladder with your kids, identifying where each of you is on the anger ladder and planning ways to encourage each other to move up the ladder.

WHEN DOES A REWARD BECOME A BRIBE?

One essential ingredient in helping to prevent discipline problems is rewarding, or showing approval, for appropriate behavior. Unfortunately, parents are always more aware of their kids' misbehaviors, because fighting, talking back, and not doing chores attracts immediate attention! However, the single most effective way to get kids to behave appropriately is to reward appropriate behavior with a deliberate, structured system of approval.

If the concept of rewarding good behavior sounds suspiciously like bribery to you, examine the discipline you received as a child. Did you receive praise for good behavior, or only criticism? Many parents were told what they did wrong as children, but not what they did right. Remember—this pattern affects your relationship with your kids. Positive reinforcement is not bribery. Bribery is rewarding inappropriate behavior hoping to get good behavior. For example, if your child is making a lot of noise while you are on the phone and you say, "Here's some dessert, please stop making all that noise," then you have rewarded inappropriate behavior.

PRINCIPLES OF REWARDS

Several important principles of rewards are important to remember:

1. Rewards are actions or things which follow a behavior and serve to strengthen it.

2. Rewards can be tangible or intangible. Tangible rewards are things which can be eaten, played with, held, touched, etc. Activities can also be considered tangible rewards. Verbal praise is an example of an intangible reward.

3. Catch your child being good. Look for opportunities to reward your kid.

4. Different strokes for different folks! To offer rewards that are

meaningful, you need to know your child and begin wherever he or she is.

For example, when our son Matt was in the first grade, we gave him a star for every page he read in a book; nine stars and he got a piece of sugarless gum, along with lots of verbal praise. In the fourth grade at school, for each book read, his rocket ship on the class chart got closer to the moon. In high school, he went to the library on his own to learn about goats because he had a goat. Matt grew from needing an immediate, tangible reward to being rewarded from within, but it took time to reach this point. Growth does not happen overnight.

GOOD REWARD TECHNIQUES

One tried-and-true technique for rewards is called "Marbles in the Jar." Get a small jar and some marbles. When you catch your child being good, say, "I really like the way you finished your chores after school without being reminded. Let's put 5 marbles in the jar." Always use verbal praise when putting marbles in the jar, and be sure to be specific in your

(Continued on next page.)

(Continued from previous page.)

praise. Be generous, and do not ever take marbles out of the jar. (Use only one jar, no matter how many children you have.) When the jar gets full, do something fun together as a family, choosing from a list of activities to which the whole family has contributed.

We used this technique for about six years in our family, sometimes filling the jar within a week or two when our children were young, and taking two to three weeks as they got older. An added bonus: you can reward all family members for being positive to each other, and the whole family will benefit from filling the jar. Parents can also praise each other and join in the fun by adding marbles. This technique even helped me remember to praise my children, since I did not receive praise from my father as a child.

A good variation of this activity for older children involves the same technique as "Marble in the Jar," but uses quarters instead of marbles. When the jar is full, spend the quarters on a family activity.

Another technique that works well to reinforce a child's good behavior is to draw a simple picture of something he or she wants to earn. Divide the picture into small squares. Each time the desired behavior is observed, you or your child colors in one or more squares. (Be sure to always accompany this action with verbal praise.) When the entire picture is colored in, purchase the object together.

A CHALLENGE TO YOU:

1. Did you receive praise or rewards as a child?

2. What behaviors could you begin to praise your child for?

3. What rewards would your child like to work for?

CHORES: IT'S EASIER TO DO IT MYSELF!

I saw a cartoon once that said, "Excusing children of responsibilities is child abuse that does not show up until adulthood."

Do your children have chores? And do they complete their chores without reminders from you? Completing chores will help children to develop responsibility and accountability. Inevitably, when I talk to a young person who is not following through with homework or school work, I'll find a student who is not being held accountable for chores at home.

BENEFITS OF CHORES

Accomplishing chores on a regular basis instills a sense of accomplishment in kids and can also enhance their self-esteem. When parents have to constantly remind their kids to finish chores, kids may learn to expect reminders from teachers, and only complete assignments when reminded or nagged.

Completing chores will also teach children how to be sympathetic to other family members. Letting kids know that you appreciate their efforts because it helps you out and saves you time will help teach them to be responsive to others and considerate of the needs of others.

CONSIDER REWARDS

Consider giving kids an allowance as a tangible reward for completing chores. An allowance can help them learn the value of money, and with a little help from you, they can

begin to learn how to budget it to meet their needs. Learning to make money and to use money wisely can create for kids a feeling that they can make things happen in their lives. (Many teenagers simply *let* things happen in their lives rather than actually trying to *make* things happen.)

The amount of an allowance needs to be comfortable for you, and meaningful for your child. Start with a small amount, increasing it as your child grows up. As the allowance amount increases, your child should be expected to assume more responsibility for his or her needs.

Kids should also be expected to do some work around the house without pay, simply because they are part of a family.

TIPS

Consider the following tips in setting up chores:

1. Write a list of all the possible chores that need to be done in the family, and as a group, divide up chores.

2. Don't discourage volunteers. If someone would rather clean a bathroom than wash dishes, try to honor that request.

3. List the chores on a chart and display the chart. Kids can mark off completion of items on the chart. If you have a home computer, make up a weekly chart; put your child in charge of printing it out and updating it.

    Continue the chart throughout high school, as it helps kids to remember the chores, serves

(Continued on next page.)

(Continued from previous page.)

as a method of accountability, and cuts down on the tendency for kids to say they "forgot."

4. Reward the completion of chores. Consider giving kids a certain amount of money as allowance (simply because they are part of the family) and additional money for each chore completed.

A "when/then" policy may also be helpful. If all chores are done on time, then all is well, but if a certain number of chores are not completed, then the offender loses a privilege (such as watching TV that night) and/or goes to bed early.

5. For chores that may be done any time during the week, pick a certain day by which they must be completed. Consequences for not finishing tasks by the deadline could include completion the following day without pay. It's important not to revert to nagging and reminding your child, but to state the rules and the consequences, and then follow through.

I remember when our son was not doing his chores during his senior year in high school. We set a new rule that if the chores were not done by Thursday night, then he could not go out on the weekend. His first question to me about this new rule was, "Could you remind me?" I said no, and several minutes later while in his room, I noticed he had posted two signs in his room, one on his window and one on his door, reminding himself to do his chores. This is the goal you are striving for—to help your kids to become responsible for themselves, instead of depending on reminders from authority figures.

A CHALLENGE TO YOU:

1. Determine whether or not you have gotten into the habit of nagging and reminding your kids to complete chores.

2. Set up chores for your kids following the tips given, and/or revise your current system to make it more effective.

WHAT IS DISCIPLINE?

The Bible gives a great deal of insight and advice about effective parenting. As we seek to parent our children in healthy and positive ways, how do we reconcile verses such as the following in our blueprint for positive parenting?

"He who spares the rod hates his son, but he who loves him is careful to discipline him" (Proverbs 13:24).

"A gentle answer turns away wrath, but a harsh word stirs up anger" (Proverbs 15:1).

"Train a child in the way he should go, and when he is old he will not turn from it" (Proverbs 22:6).

"Love is patient, love is kind" (1 Corinthians 13:4).

"Do everything in love" (1 Corinthians 16:14).

"Fathers, do not exasperate your children; instead, bring them up in the training and instruction of the Lord" (Ephesians 6:4).

"For you know that we dealt with each of you as a father deals with his own children, encouraging, comforting and urging you to live lives worthy of God" (1 Thessalonians 2:11).

"Therefore encourage one another and build each other up, just as in fact you are doing" (1 Thessalonians 5:11).

"Everyone should be quick to listen, slow to speak and slow to become angry" (James 1: 19b).

Many parents consider discipline to be synonymous with punishment, but it is not. Discipline is training that enables a young person to make appropriate choices in a climate of warmth and support.

THE ABC'S OF DISCIPLINE

The ABC's of discipline are: Antecedents—Behaviors—Consequences.

As parents, we tend to look at our children's misbehavior and then wonder what consequences, penalties or punishment to apply to change that behavior. But to reduce the number and frequency of misbehaviors, and to create a positive home climate, we need to concentrate on the antecedents of (the things that came before) the misbehaviors. Simply put, when kids do not feel loved, are not listened to, and do not receive

approval for appropriate behaviors, their tendency to misbehave will be much greater.

Now, imagine a bowl of fruit. Think of the bowl as discipline. Think of the fruit in the bowl as love, sympathy, approval and punishment/correction. The essential ingredients to a positive approach to parenting is one that includes all four components.

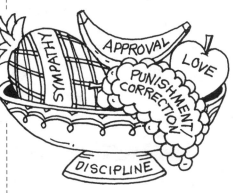

A short summary of the first three essential ingredients will be helpful before we discuss punishment or corrective measures when a child misbehaves (the topic of a future article).

LOVE

Love needs to be unconditional, and it needs to be expressed to your child in his or her language of love. All young people need eye contact, physical

(Continued on next page.)

(Continued from previous page.)

contact and focused attention. They need you to tune in to their language of love. If they want pizza when you take them out to dinner, don't take them to a hamburger joint. If they'd like to go to a movie, don't take them bowling. Showing love to your children in the above fashion will help them feel valued, which in turn will result in less misbehavior.

SYMPATHY

Sympathy involves really listening to and accepting your kids' feelings—especially their feelings of anger. It means attempting to comfort them when they are hurting. *Listen* when your children talk to you; don't immediately start giving advice, don't tell them why they shouldn't feel that way, and don't feel you have to do something to solve their problems. Simply listening solves many problems.

APPROVAL

Approval involves praise and/or other rewards for appropriate behavior. When you praise your kids, be sure to look at them, move close to them, be specific with your praise, and praise them frequently. Setting up tangible rewards for achieving specific goals will also motivate kids to achieve goals.

When kids are punished for misbehavior, they know what they shouldn't do, but do not necessarily learn what they *should* do. Approval for appropriate behavior is how they will learn that behavior.

Did you receive love, sympathy and approval as a child? If not, you may have to make a more conscious, deliberate effort to use these tools in your family. You may even feel awkward when you first begin to apply these strategies, but don't give up. Time, practice and patience will make use of these tools feel more natural.

A CHALLENGE TO YOU:

1. Which of the three tools (love, sympathy, approval) do you need to use more in your family?

2. Choose specific strategies you will use to apply these tools and create a more positive home climate (let my child choose an outing, begin the "Marbles in a Jar" technique, etc.).

WHAT SHOULD I DO WHEN MY PRETEEN MISBEHAVES?
(PART 1 OF 2)

All children and teenagers *will* need correction or punishment when they misbehave. The question to answer is not *whether* punishment or correction is needed, but what punishment is needed for each offense and for each child.

I used to think that it did not matter *why* kids misbehaved. One could simply apply a punishment and change the behavior. However, experience proved me wrong! It is very important to consider the *why* of a young person's misbehavior.

Kids may misbehave for a variety of reasons: because they are tired, bored, hungry; they may simply be testing the limits (all youngsters need and want limits, but they will still test them); they may be stressed; they may be demonstrating anger in a passive-aggressive way; they may be trying to escape work beyond their capabilities; they may have a physical problem such as Attention Deficit Disorder with or without Hyperactivity. It is very important to determine the reason or reasons your preteen is misbehaving—otherwise you will not know the correct approach to take.

CLARIFY AND FOLLOW THROUGH

A word of prevention: Two of the quickest ways to lose control as a parent are ground rules that are unclear, and inconsistent follow-through. Parents and kids both *must* clearly understand the rules, as well as the consequences that will follow broken rules. Rules need to be specified as either (1) mandatory—rules you as a parent will follow through on, or (2) discretionary—areas that you have turned over to your child.

As kids mature, begin to turn over areas to their judgment. At some point, let kids decide their bedtimes, the state of their rooms, what time they do homework, etc. Obviously, if the child is not able to make appropriate decisions, those areas need to come back under parental control. When parents themselves cannot agree about rules, or when they do not or cannot enforce rules, there will be a great deal of stress and disharmony in the home.

Next, I will describe three punishment techniques; several others will be discussed in the next article, Part 2.

PUNISHMENT TECHNIQUES

The first, a technique many think is reserved for the two-year-old throwing a temper tantrum, works very well at this age level: **Ignore it!** You might be amazed at how much better a day goes if you can ignore one or two things your child says or does during the day. On a shopping trip with her mom, our oldest daughter began to complain that she didn't get to have lunch out after getting a haircut and buying some clothes. My wife ignored her remarks and several minutes

(Continued on next page.)

• 5th & 6th Grade Smart Pages • 111

(Continued from previous page.)

later when they got in the car, Robyn said, "Thanks, Mom. I had a great time!"

Ignored behavior often gets worse before it gets better, so hang in there even when it seems not to be working. But don't ignore inappropriate behaviors for a period of months; instead, move toward establishing consequences.

Mild social punishment is another technique designed to nip a potentially troublesome situation in the bud. Move close to the offender and state in a firm voice, "Stop that right now. I do not like it when you (talk back, fight with your sister, talk back to me)." Do not launch into a lecture, but be brief and to the point in your comments. For some kids, this will be enough of a consequence to eliminate the misbehavior.

A third punishment strategy can be found in Luke 15, Jesus' parable of the Lost Son. When one son asked for his inheritance, the father gave it to him, probably knowing full well that the son would make mistakes. When the son returned after having spent all of his money, his father welcomed him home. The son had learned a valuable lesson. Most parents want to tell their kids what to do and what not to do, rather than allowing them to experience a **logical consequence** to their misbehavior.

When using logical consequences, calmly state the rule and the consequences, and calmly follow through when the rule is broken. For instance, if your child consistently leaves clothes or toys out, put them in a "Saturday Bag," and allow them to purchase the items on the following Saturday. If your preteen comes home 15 minutes late, have that child come home 15 minutes earlier the next time he or she goes out. If dirty clothes can't find their way into a hamper, do not wash them. If kids waste money and do not have money for a special event, the consequences would be missing that event. Oversleeping means being tardy at school. Not every misbehavior has a logical consequence; however, plenty of situations warrant this technique.

Always consider your child's temperament when implementing a punishment. For some kids, a stern look will be punishment enough. For others, the loss of a privilege will be necessary to teach a lesson. And even the above techniques will not be enough to deal with all situations! So in the next article, I'll describe several other punishment strategies including a **fine system**, **grounding**, and the **X chart system**.

A CHALLENGE TO YOU:

1. Think of one or two misbehaviors that you could simply ignore, and try that technique.

2. Think of a specific misbehavior with a logical consequence that you could implement.

3. Examine your childhood experiences. What punishment strategies did your parents use? What were the results?

WHAT SHOULD i DO WHEN MY PRETEEN MISBEHAVES?
(PART 2 OF 2)

A rule of thumb: When a child misbehaves, it is very important to *calmly* state the rule and the consequence, and then follow through consistently. Often, parents use anger and emotion to try to control their kids' behavior, but it's very inappropriate and ineffective. Imagine if a traffic cop stopped you for speeding and was ranting and raving, losing his cool; you might end up with a ticket, but you'd leave with a lack of respect for the officer. So it is when parents yell and scream as they apply punishment strategies.

Another important principle to consider: In changing a child's behavior, it may take a month for every year of your child's age to make real change take hold. If your child is 10 years old, it may take 10 months to really change the behavior. You will probably see some progress sooner, but parents typically err in thinking that behaviors will change faster. Consequently, they may skip around, trying and discarding many disciplinary techniques instead of sticking to techniques for a longer period of time.

A fourth punishment technique* is establishment of a **fine system**. When failure to put a new roll of toilet paper in the holder became an issue in our family, I informed my three kids that if it was not done, they would each be fined 50 cents. Naturally, they all said, "Thanks Dad, for holding us accountable!" Wrong! They said it wasn't fair because "what if it wasn't their fault?" I simply explained that they could help one another. I give this example to show that kids will complain about your rules and will try to get out of consequences. Don't get thrown off guard by their countermoves; expect them—then just

FINES

follow through calmly with the consequence. Fines can work well in situations where young people are disrespectful, swear, put down a sibling, or leave clothes or items around the house.

Grounding for short periods of time can also be an effective punishment for some misbehaviors. Start with a short time period, increasing time only if the shorter time is not effective. Make sure you can enforce the grounding if you use this as a consequence. Consider giving time off the sentence if your preteen is willing to do some manual labor to help you around the house or yard.

Another very effective punishment strategy is the **assertive discipline system** or **X chart**. This system works well on behaviors such as talking back, fighting among siblings, being disrespectful, interrupting while you are on the phone, etc. Try to deal with only one behavior at a time.

Set up a chart as follows: List consequences across the top of the chart that are meaningful to your child. (Several examples appear on the sample chart

---

*See previous article for the first three techniques: **ignoring** the behavior, **mild social punishment** and **logical consequences**.

(Continued on next page.)

(Continued from previous page.)

shown on next page.) When your child demonstrates the targeted misbehavior, simply state the rule and tell him or her you are putting an *X* on the chart. The first *X* on that day means a warning, the second one on the same day means loss of the first privilege, and so on until an early bedtime.

It's important to always have the chart available, even though you may not need to use it very often. In fact, if this system is working well you may have only two or three *X*s on the chart each week. The system can be used when you are driving in a car or out at a restaurant. Simply remind your child of the chart and state that you will record *X*s later for misbehavior.

While a very effective technique for young children (less than five years old) and in danger of hurting themselves (running into the street), **physical punishment** or **spanking** is not an effective technique to use when kids are older. For one thing, preteens are much more likely and able to flee parents who use physical punishment. For another, preteens can turn on their parents in a physical manner, escalating a spiral of physical violence. Many other strategies are more effective in teaching children to make appropriate choices in a climate of warmth and support. If parents use punishment strategies that are too severe or too punitive, kids will learn not to come to that parent for help or advice. They will also be motivated to lie to avoid those punitive consequences.

Remember, for punishment strategies to be effective, you must also practice strategies covered in previous letters: showing unconditional love, listening to your child, helping him or her deal effectively with anger, praising and rewarding appropriate behaviors, and setting up an effective chore chart system.

	Warning	Dessert	Play with a friend	TV	Go to bed early
Monday					
Tuesday					
Wednesday					
Thursday					
Friday					
Saturday					
Sunday					

A CHALLENGE TO YOU:

1. Review and implement the strategies discussed in previous articles before implementing any of the punishment strategies listed in this article.

2. Set up the assertive discipline chart or use the fine system for a specific misbehavior. State the rule and the consequence and follow through calmly and consistently.

PROBLEMS IN SCHOOL

There are many reasons why kids may have difficulties in school. Really listen to your child if he or she is complaining about something at school. When you hear, "I hate school!" try to uncover specific reasons for those feelings. Instead of closing off conversation with, "Don't worry, it will get better," encourage your child to keep talking by saying something like, "School seems like it isn't going too well, is it?"

One must know the reasons that a child is having trouble in school in order to arrive at the correct solution to the problem. Kids may exhibit academic as well as behavioral problems in school if they: have below-average intellectual ability or are very gifted; are in the wrong grade; have a learning disability; are bored; or have Attention Deficit Disorder with or without Hyperactivity.

DISCOVER REASONS

If your child is experiencing difficulties in school, it's essential to have him or her evaluated by the school psychologist or a Licensed Educational Psychologist. The evaluation should include a full-scale intelligence test (the WISC-Third Edition is probably best at this age), an achievement test, fine motor skills tests, and visual perception testing. These tests will identify most of the reasons previously mentioned.

If kids have **poor nutrition**, lots of sugar or caffeine, they may also experience difficulties in school. A healthy, well-balanced diet is important for school success.

Some kids are not motivated by their parents to **set goals**. Make every effort to help your child set goals that are meaningful and reasonable to achieve in the time period available. When goals are not achieved, help them to maintain a positive attitude and revise the goals as necessary. Reward

their efforts toward achieving the goals, not only the attainment of those goals. Give a great deal of encouragement along the way.

Inconsistent rule enforcement at school and/or at home often results in misbehavior at school. Also, many kids who do not have chores and responsibilities at home find it difficult to

complete their work at school. Kids not only need chores and responsibilities at home, but they need to be held accountable if the chores are not completed. If parents rely too much on nagging and reminding, kids will count on teachers to do the same thing at school.

Some kids will misbehave at school if the **expectations of teachers and/or parents are unrealistic**. When kids feel they can't achieve what is expected of them, they may misbehave to get out of the situation. Make sure your expectations are realistic for your child. The psychological testing discussed previously can help you set realistic expectations.

When a family or child is under a great deal of **stress**, behavior and academic efforts may reflect this stress. One common stressor is the experience of many changes in the family in a short amount of time. For example, if the parents have divorced, a child may have to move or spend time at two households, a parent may have to go back to work, different child care may be required, etc. Sometimes, the passing of time and discussion of the issues is all that will help.

When kids are **unable to express their anger in healthy ways**, they may resort to a passive-aggressive way of expressing it. Kids demonstrating anger in a passive-aggressive fashion may fail

(Continued on next page.)

(Continued from previous page.)

to turn in assignments or to study, may dawdle and procrastinate in doing their work, and may "lose" assignments. Most kids really have no idea that what they are doing is expressing anger in a way that makes the teacher and/or parent angry, but is really hurting only themselves. At home and in school, adults should encourage and teach kids to express their anger in healthy ways.

Typically, if all of the above areas have been explored and the problem remains, then one may suspect a child having difficulty in school of having Attention Deficit Disorder. However, ADD is generally diagnosed around the first or second grade; it's not a problem that suddenly develops when a kid is 10 or 11.

GET INVOLVED

Regardless of the academic and/or behavior problems that your child may be experiencing,

it's extremely important for you to be involved in the education of your kids. Your attendance at parent-teacher conferences, volunteering to help at school, and asking the teacher what you can do at home will all help your child to be successful in school. Show confidence in your child's teacher and support the school (from an informed viewpoint, of course).

In some school situations, it can be very beneficial to set up a school-to-home communication system. With your child's teacher, decide on four to five specific behaviors that you'd like your child to achieve in school. List all the items (complete math assignments, follow teacher's directions, raise hand before talking, etc.) and add two columns to the list, one headed with the word "yes" and the other headed with the word "no."

Each day the teacher checks yes or no for each behavior, then

totals the two columns, and the child takes the form home to be signed by you and returned the next day. Make up a contract rewarding the positive behavior. For instance, if the child earns at least four out of five positive marks, he or she may watch TV, earn a small amount of money, or play with friends. If the child has not earned the agreed-upon amount, he or she is grounded for that day; the next day start the process over. Also include a long-term reinforcer, such as, when the child earns 40 or 50 positive marks, a friend may spend the night, or you will take him or her on an outing.

This system can be very successful in helping you and the school work closely together, and in assisting your child to achieve his or her potential, since expectations of the teacher, the parents and the child are made very clear to all parties involved.

A CHALLENGE TO YOU:

1. If your child is experiencing some difficulties in school, consider all the possible reasons listed above.

2. Set up the school-to-home communication system if your child is experiencing consistent behavior and/or academic problems in school.

i GET TOO ANGRY AT MY KIDS

Several years ago, I counseled a woman with a 12-year-old son who was having academic as well as behavior problems at home and in school. None of my suggestions seemed to work. The mother had trouble setting up chore charts, she could not find fun things to do with her son, she had trouble praising him for appropriate behaviors, and she had trouble listening to his problems. Nothing seemed to work. Then one day, she said, "I say every hateful thing to my son that I would like to say to my brother!" In her family of origin, her brother was the one with all the problems, the one that made life miserable for everyone. At that moment, I became aware of the hidden factors that can keep parents from applying their parenting tools calmly, effectively and consistently.

UNRESOLVED RESENTMENT

If you have unresolved resentment toward anyone in your past, you may bring that old anger into the present, and become too angry at your children. Over many years of counseling experience, I have noticed that fathers often tend to feel that their childhood has not affected their ability to be a good parent; mothers tend to look more at their childhoods, but may think they have dealt with all the issues in their pasts, when, in reality, they have not dealt with the issues sufficiently.

The Bible is very clear on the importance of forgiving others. In fact, God states that if we do not forgive others, we will not be for-

given. One common problem is that we may say we have forgiven someone, but we may not actually spend enough time discussing, crying about and sharing our pain in order to really heal the hurts of the past. If you have not forgiven people that hurt you in the past, you may reassign all that anger to someone in the present, and consequently overreact to his or her behavior. Working through unresolved resentments and forgiving those that have hurt us can take a lifetime, but it is extremely important. Your happiness and the well-being of your child is at stake.

FAMILIAR PATTERNS

Some parents overreact and become too angry at their kids because that seems normal to them. They are doing to their children exactly what was done to them. Often, these parents tell me that they do not want to yell, scream and nag like their parents did to them. Simply recognizing what they are doing is a major step toward creating a more positive home climate and using parenting strategies effectively, consistently and calmly.

UNREALISTIC EXPECTATIONS

Another cause for parents' anger: Most children and teenagers do not live up to their parents' expectations. In this case, the anger may have little to do with the child and more to do with unrealistic expectations; nevertheless it can create real problems in parenting. If you have unrealistic expectations, expecting all *As*

(Continued on next page.)

(Continued from previous page.)

when a child's potential is *B*- or *C*-level work, then you may tend to overreact when low grades are received.

GRIEF

Whenever one experiences a loss (your child gets a *C* average, not the *A* average you expected; he goes out for football instead of band, she gets suspended from school, etc.) a parent needs to work through the stages of grief. The stages of grief are: confusion, denial, anger/guilt, depression, understanding and acceptance. Acceptance does not mean that you allow negative behavior to remain, but only when you reach understanding and acceptance will you be able to help your child. If you get stuck at the stage of anger or guilt or depression, or never move past denial, then you will not be able to parent in a healthy way, and your child will suffer.

Usually one only considers grieving as needed when a person dies. However, it is important for parents to identify their feelings of sadness, anger, hurt and guilt about their children's losses and failures, as well, and to discuss their feelings, and realize the importance of working through these feelings.

INTERPRETATION

Another factor that will cause parents to become too angry and overemotional has to do with how they interpret their child's misbehavior. If your child misbehaves and you think he or she did it deliberately to make you mad, then you will probably get mad.

If you think or say the word "should" regarding your child's behavior, then your resulting emotion will usually be an overreaction when the desired behavior does not happen. For example, if you say to yourself, "My son should do his chores," and the chores do not get done, then you will probably be too angry to deal with the misbehavior in a healthy, positive, calm fashion. When one commands someone to do something and the behavior does not occur; one tends to become overemotional.

God gave us all choices. He has spelled out the consequences to our not following the Commandments, but has allowed us to make the choice. So it is that parents need to spell out consequences, but allow their kids to make choices. It would be healthier to state or feel, "I would like it if my son would choose to complete his chores, but he may test me, or simply decide that it would be more fun to play." If the child does not complete the chores, parents need to invoke the consequences, or change the consequences to something more severe so that the child will make the more appropriate choice the next time.

A CHALLENGE TO YOU:

1. Which of the reasons above best describes why you might overreact or become too angry when dealing with your child?

2. Take some time to deal with that explanation. Talk about it with others, grieve losses as needed, and work actively to forgive anyone who has hurt you in the past.

PARENTS: IS YOUR LIFE IN BALANCE?

Evaluate what you rely on to help yourself feel a purpose in life. Look back over recent weeks. What have you relied on to help you feel good about yourself? When your child comes home from school with an *F* on a test, do you feel that you have received an *F* in parenting? When your child wins an award, do you feel like you've won, too?

Many parents rely totally on their children for self-esteem. Others rely on their careers for their satisfaction. It's dangerous and unhealthy to rely on only one or two areas of life for a sense of personal worth. To parent well, we must constantly strive for balance in life.

As a Christian, I know that I am worthwhile, no matter what. My self-worth does not depend on what I do, or how many people I counsel with in a day, or what my young adults are doing with their lives. Since God has created me in his image, I am worthwhile no matter what I do. In other words, God loves me unconditionally. I don't have to earn His love. Acceptance of God's unconditional love forms a basis for a healthy balance in life.

IS YOUR LIFE IN BALANCE? CONSIDER THE FOLLOWING FACETS OF YOUR LIFE:

◆ **SPIRITUAL:** Do you regularly attend church? Are you working on building a personal relationship with God?

◆ **PHYSICAL:** Do you exercise? Are you watching what you eat and drink? Do you take time to relax?

◆ **PROFESSIONAL:** (This may relate to your work inside the home or outside the home.) How do you feel about this component of your life?

◆ **MARITAL:** How do you feel about your marriage relationship? If you are not married, evaluate your relationships with others.

◆ **SOCIAL:** Do you go out with others? With whom do you socialize? Are they positive influences in your life or do they tend to drag you down or depress you?

◆ **PERSONAL GROWTH:** Have you sought out any resources recently to help you with relationships or your own self-esteem?

◆ **FINANCIAL:** How would you rate your financial situation? Are you spending more money than you make?

◆ **PARENTAL:** How do you feel about your relationship with your children?

Now rate each area of your life on a scale from 1 to 10. See chart next page. (1, 2 or 3 means you are in the pits; 4, 5 or 6 means you are in the average range; 7, 8, 9 or 10 means you are soaring in that area.) This is a very subjective test, but it can shed a great deal of light on your life.

(Continued on next page.)

• 5th & 6th Grade Smart Pages • 119

(Continued from previous page.)

SPIRITUAL	1	2	3	4	5	6	7	8	9	10
PHYSICAL	1	2	3	4	5	6	7	8	9	10
PROFESSIONAL	1	2	3	4	5	6	7	8	9	10
MARITAL	1	2	3	4	5	6	7	8	9	10
SOCIAL	1	2	3	4	5	6	7	8	9	10
PERSONAL GROWTH	1	2	3	4	5	6	7	8	9	10
FINANCIAL	1	2	3	4	5	6	7	8	9	10
PARENTAL	1	2	3	4	5	6	7	8	9	10

When one's life is out of balance, one will tend to be much more affected by disappointments in a particular area. If you are attempting to get all of your sense of worth or relief from stress from one or two areas, your well-being will be seriously threatened. You may overreact and become too angry if those one or two areas are not going well.

One woman I counseled with felt really good only if her husband was happy, and his happiness was dependent on whether or not he was making lots of sales in real estate. He was too dependent on a shaky real estate market, and she was too dependent on him and his mood.

Another man I counseled with rated himself in the pits in all areas listed. His idea of improving his life was to double his salary in two months. He knew this wouldn't happen, but he was focusing on that one area to the detriment of the rest. I said to him, "If you walk to church with your family on Sunday, you will be helping to balance the spiritual, physical, social, marital, and parental aspects of your life, and that is something you *can* do." He never returned to counseling. He was stuck, focusing on only one area of his life, the financial area, hoping that if it changed, all would be well. John Wooden, the famous UCLA coach, once said, "Don't let what you *can't* do keep you from doing what you *can* do."

One added benefit to achieving balance in your life is that you'll be modeling powerful life skills for your children. With time and patience, you'll be helping to equip your kids with a very important tool for a healthy adult life. With balance in their lives, kids will handle disappointments much better and have a healthier self-esteem.

A CHALLENGE TO YOU:

1. Pick out the three areas you rated lowest, and write out specific goals to improve those areas.

2. Rate the same areas of your spouse's life, and have him or her rate your life. Complete this exercise by discussing the evaluations.

Do You Want A Better Relationship With Your Preteen?

Most parents (unless they need a course in honesty), would answer an emphatic "yes" to the above question. However, since parents often do not know how to improve their relationships with their kids, they refrain from asking themselves the question.

John Kennedy, in the 1960s, did not figure out how to get a man on the moon—he just felt it was a goal worth pursuing. Once the country bought the goal, it was accomplished. In other words, don't let the lack of knowing how to improve your relationship with your kids deter you from deciding that you would like your relationships to be better. When you decide you want things to get better, and accept your role in making that happen, then it *can* happen.

If you want to improve the relationships in your life, the answer is simple. The solution, however, will take work, require you to take risks and will be stressful. You'll need to do something *different*. (Someone once said that the definition of insanity is doing the same thing over and over, hoping for different results!)

Three Ways To Improve

There are three general ways to improve your relationship with your kids. You can:

1. Stop doing things that take joy out of your life. This includes: comparing yourself to others, going on guilt trips, continuing to harbor resentments toward someone in your past, and maintaining a stress-producing schedule.

2. Continue doing things that you have already been doing that bring more satisfaction in your relationships. Many parents begin a great routine of taking a child out to lunch or dinner, or letting them decide what they want to do on a "date" night with you, only to "run out of steam" and stop doing these positive things.

3. Do some *new* things that may bring more love and joy in your life. This one is probably the most difficult, for it involves taking a risk—the risk of trying something new and continuing to apply it, even in the face of opposition or resistance from your preteen.

This scenario fits a variety of parenting situations: for instance, starting up a chore chart system, trying to give your kids more physical affection, trying to be more sympathetic to them, etc. All change is uncomfortable, and many parents will hit the discomfort zone and quickly go back to the old, familiar ways because they seem more comfortable. When you hit this spot, remind yourself that you can't reach a better place

(Continued on next page.)

(Continued from previous page.)

without working through this uncomfortable zone.

DO IT NOW

There are some more good reasons for making changes in your parenting techniques *now*, during your child's preteen years. Typically, when parents begin to experience difficulties with their kids, they will tend to blame the kids for the problems instead of looking at themselves and their parenting tools.

It's very important to revise your parenting approaches now if you are to be effective in parenting a teenager. Approaches that were successful with a 5-year-old will probably not be very effective with a 15-year-old. Also, during this calm time period prior to the teen years, kids are generally more easygoing and much more receptive to hearing from mom and dad. When the teen years hit, peer pressure—both the positive and negative aspects of it—become much more influential on a child, and parents' influence becomes less effective.

BE PATIENT

Someone once asked a speaker what was the most important thing to remember in parenting through the teen years. His answer was simple, but profound: Remember that teenagers are like asparagus, not radishes. Radishes begin to produce an edible product within weeks after the seed is planted; but when asparagus is planted, it needs to be patiently nurtured for two to four years before it begins to produce an edible food. Be patient and remember that teenagers are like asparagus, not radishes.

Successful parenting through the preteen and teenage years is not a matter of luck. It involves learning the correct tools or parenting strategies, and dealing with hidden factors in your own life that can interfere with the consistent and effective application of the parenting strategies. This series of articles is designed to help you evaluate your current parenting strategies, discard ineffective ones, and establish more effective techniques.

A CHALLENGE TO YOU:

1. Have you done the same things to your child as was done to you as a child? Or have you done the complete opposite because you hated what was done to you?

2. Do you accept the need to learn appropriate strategies to be effective as a parent?

WHAT KIND OF MODEL ARE YOU?

I'll never forget the woman who came to counseling several years ago regarding problems she was having with her 11-year-old son. At one particular session, she was very frustrated and angry with her son because he would not wear his seat belt while riding in the car. I can occasionally ask silly questions, but this time I hit on a good one and asked if *she* had worn her seat belt while driving. She said no, but that her son should do what she said, and he should know it's important to wear a seat belt. This parent clearly did not fully comprehend the importance of being a good model to her son!

Another parent I counseled with was very frustrated that his six-year-old boy was hitting other children at school. The man related how every day that he got a report from school saying his son had hit another student, he would spank his son. He could not figure out why his son's behavior was not changing. He did not realize he was modeling that physical force was the correct way to deal with a problem.

But recognizing poor modeling is the beginning of healthier parenting techniques. Here's an example. When Robyn, my oldest

daughter, was about five, I yelled at her to quit yelling. My wife, Pam, said, "I don't think this is going to work!" It dawned on me that I was demonstrating the same behavior I wanted her to stop. Later on, we set up a system whereby Robyn gave me a penny when she yelled at us, and I gave her a dime when I yelled at her. It worked like a charm, and we had fun catching each other and collecting the money, until both of our behaviors changed for the good.

PRACTICE IT

In spite of the fact that nearly all parents recognize the importance of being good models, many, many parents do not put this concept into practice on a daily basis. What are you modeling for your kids? Do you yell and scream? Do you put off doing projects until the last minute? Do you pick up after yourself? Do you say "please" and "thank you"? Do you express your anger in a positive, healthy fashion? Make a conscious effort to note what you are

modeling to your kids, and realize the significance of your own behavior.

During a recent vacation, my wife and I and our three kids were driving through the desert when the car's air conditioner suddenly stopped working. As we endured 110-degree heat, I remember being very much aware of what I needed to model for my children. Yelling, swearing, blaming our mechanic, and blaming my wife all came to my mind as normal responses. However, I knew that demonstrating these behaviors would not serve as a good model for my children to

(Continued on next page.)

(Continued from previous page.)

reflect on when they were faced with such a problem. Instead, we discussed how we could get the car fixed in the next town, arranged to get a rental car and found a shop to repair the air conditioner. We will always remember that trip, and I am thankful I was able to model appropriate coping strategies.

EXPLAIN IT

Another very important aspect of modeling is to *tell* kids when you are modeling something you want kids to learn. Don't leave it up to chance. Don't just assume your kids will observe your positive behavior and begin to copy it. If you have to get a report out at work by Friday, and it's ready by Wednesday, say to your kid, "I have to get a report done by Friday, but I've already got it done and it's only Wednesday." If you are trying to fix something around the house or yard you can say, "This job may take a while and it's frustrating, but I'm going to stick to it until it's done." Let your kids know when you are doing something you'd like them to do.

That guideline holds true on the interpersonal level, too: If a friend hurts your feelings, you can tell your child what happened by saying, "My friend really hurt my feelings by what he did, but I talked with him, and we worked things out." Describe how you forgave the person that hurt you. Help your kids realize that holding on to anger is not healthy. When appropriate, let them know of people you have had to forgive in the past.

ADMIT IT

When you make a mistake, let your kids know. They need to see their parents admit mistakes, and they need to realize that their parents are not perfect. When you are sad, let your kids hear you express your sadness through your words and your tears. By modeling these emotions and the appropriate ways to express them, you will help your kids learn how to deal with disappointment.

A CHALLENGE TO YOU:

1. What behaviors did your parents model for you that were appropriate? inappropriate?

2. What behaviors are you modeling for your children that are not appropriate?

3. What behaviors are you modeling for your children that are appropriate? Remember to call those to their attention.

ENHANCING YOUR CHILD'S SELF-ESTEEM
(PART 1 OF 2)

If there were just two things that I could give to my children, two things that would assure their place in the world and set them up for life, one would be a positive, daily relationship with our Father in Heaven, and the second would be a healthy self-esteem. The two can go hand in hand as we feel and appreciate God's unconditional love for us.

Self-esteem gauges how a person feels about him- or herself. It's the confidence of knowing one's worth as a human being, coupled with a healthy concern to maintain that posture. For kids, the way they feel about themselves will affect the friends they pick, the quality of their schoolwork and the amount of risks they will be able to take. Also, most importantly, it will affect how they deal with the problems of negative peer pressure that are extremely challenging in the preteen and teen years. Fortunately, there are some very specific things you can do to enhance your preteen's self-esteem.

1. SHOW UNCONDITIONAL LOVE TO YOUR CHILD.

Convey the same kind of love that God shows us. He loves us no matter what we do. You can convey this love verbally: "That's a great report card, but always remember that we love you no matter what you do," or "Don't worry about whether or not you score in the game today, because God and I will love you no matter what."

You can also show unconditional love by giving your child healthy doses of eye contact, physical contact and focused attention. And be sure to show your love in your child's "language of love"—if you take your child out, let him or her pick what you do when you go out. Your efforts will be much more appreciated when they are understood as love by the recipient.

Encourage your child's relationship with and trust in our Heavenly Father. Continually emphasize through words and actions that, because we were all created in God's likeness, we are all worthwhile and important, no matter what we accomplish, and no matter what failures we may experience.

2. ACCEPT YOUR PRETEEN'S FEELINGS.

One of the most common mistakes parents make is not accepting their child's feelings. When your son or daughter states, "You love my brother more than me," don't say, "No, that isn't true." Say something like, "Wow, it must make you really sad to feel we love your brother more than you. I am sorry you feel that way. Can you tell me what has led to those feelings?" In this way, you will be acknowledging your child's feelings and moving towards resolving the issues that have led to those feelings.

Accepting feelings can be very difficult—especially when those

(Continued on next page.)

(Continued from previous page.)

feelings do not make sense to us. But it's important to accept kids' feelings even when the logic they have used to arrive at those feelings does not make sense to us.

3. ALLOW YOUR PRETEEN TO MAKE AS MANY DECISIONS AS POSSIBLE.

Do not let kids decide whether or not to go to church, school or the doctor! However, there are many situations in which kids can be encouraged to make their own decisions, such as: what they will wear to school, how they will fix their hair, when they will go to bed at night, what sports they wish to participate in, what classes they want to take at school, etc.

Guide kids in decision making by discussing the pros and cons, and intervene only if those decisions have not been wise ones. For example, if you allow your child to choose a bedtime, and he or she consistently stays up so late

that he or she is late for school, then you will need to go back to setting bedtime. Permit the child's decision making to go on as long as he or she continues to make responsible decisions; take back the decision making if he or she consistently makes poor choices. Allow your kids to learn from the decisions they make. Maturity is developed in the trial-and-error process of gaining and losing responsibility for decisions.

4. PRAISE YOUR KIDS' ACHIEVEMENTS AND THEIR EFFORTS TOWARDS ACHIEVING THOSE GOALS.

I honestly believe that the points previously made are more important than praise; however, praise is a very powerful way to enhance your child's self-esteem. Make sure your praise is specific and accurately describes what your preteen has done. Tangible

rewards such as gifts, privileges and money can also be helpful in backing up your words.

5. HELP YOUR PRETEEN SET AND ACHIEVE GOALS.

When Chrissy, our youngest daughter, was five, she came home from school and said that she did not know how to jump rope very well. She asked, "Dad, will you give me a nickel for every time I can jump rope past 20 in a row?" By the end of the weekend she was up to 30 to 40 in a row, while turning a complete circle—an excellent example of setting goals and working to achieve them. Help your kids to set goals in school, in raising money towards a purchase, in finishing a project for school, in reading a certain number of books. Praise and reward not only the accomplishment of those goals, but also the progress and effort made toward achieving those goals.

A CHALLENGE TO YOU:

1. What did your parents do that affected your self-esteem in a positive way? What did they do to affect your self-esteem in a negative way?

2. Which of the three ways to show unconditional love (eye contact, physical contact and focused attention) do you need to do more of? Set up a plan to meet those goals this next week.

3. Plan a way to enhance your child's self-esteem in at least one other area (accepting feelings, making decisions, praise, or goal setting).

ENHANCING YOUR CHILD'S SELF-ESTEEM
(PART 2 OF 2)

In addition to specific strategies to help parents enhance their kids' self-esteem (listed in Part 1), it's extremely important for you, as a parent, to have high self-esteem in order to help your kids develop high self-esteem. As a parent what are you modeling for your children? Do you demonstrate high self-esteem by speaking your views assertively, taking on new challenges, being willing to listen to the views of others, and working toward personal goals? Look back at your childhood and life experiences to determine how your self-esteem was formed. If it is low; work hard to enhance your own self-esteem; then the task of building your children's self-esteem will be much easier.

Here are a few other ways you can help to enhance your kids' self-esteem:

1. EXAMINE THE VALUES IN YOUR HOME.

If you value sports and your child is not good in sports, he or she may not feel appreciated or important. My father was very good at making things with his hands; as a child, I was not good in this area, and consequently I did not receive any praise from my father. I was good in schoolwork, but that was not his strength. His lack of praise affected my self-esteem in a negative way.

Make every effort to value and support your child's values. For instance, if your child enjoys being on the swim team, go to the meets even if swimming is not very important to you. If your child is not a very good student, be sure you do not place too much value on getting straight *A*'s,

but rather, value his or her compassionate nature or interest in sports or music.

2. AVOID COMPARISONS.

To most parents, it's very obvious that one should not compare kids to each other or to other children outside the family. Realize, however, that kids will do this on their own. Make every effort possible to encourage them *not* to compare themselves to others.

3. ADMIT YOUR FAULTS AND MISTAKES.

Let your children know when you make a mistake and what your faults are. It's important for kids to realize that they do not have to be perfect, and that it's OK to make mistakes.

4. EXAMINE YOUR EXPECTATIONS.

All parents have expectations for their children. Make sure that your expectations are not too low *or* too high. When children do not achieve our expectations, it rarely occurs to them to consider that

(Continued on next page.)

(Continued from previous page.)

our expectations may not be reasonable. Instead, they only feel inadequate when they do not live up to those expectations.

5. ALLOW YOUR PRETEEN TIME TO STRUGGLE WITH ACCOMPLISHMENTS.

Someone once said, "If you do anything for your children that they can do for themselves, you are crippling them emotionally." Do not jump in right away if your child is struggling at something; instead, encourage him or her to persist. A child (and most adults, too) will feel much better having accomplished a goal through hard work.

6. DISCUSS "FLAT SPOTS" AND "ROUND SPOTS" AND HELP YOUR CHILD TO COMPENSATE.

All kids have strengths (round spots) and weaknesses (flat spots) in school and sports, as well as other areas of their lives. Help your kids to identify their flat spots, and teach them that no one is perfectly round. We all have our strengths and weaknesses, and good self-esteem does not mean we are perfectly round, but that we accept our flat spots and strive to work hard in those areas, not give up on them.

More importantly, children need to be taught ways to **compensate** for their weaknesses. If your preteen has poor handwriting, encourage him to learn to type; if she is poor in spelling, teach her to use a spelling checker on the computer. I have evaluated many kids with school problems who were very bright, but developed negative views of themselves because too much effort was concentrated on helping them to improve their flat spots instead of allowing them to develop ways to compensate. Encourage kids to work hard to remediate flat spots *and* to use techniques to help compensate for those flat spots.

The sequence just described (identifying flat spots, reinforcing strengths, and finding ways to compensate for weaknesses) is a long process, and it takes time and patience.

7. CHORES DEVELOP CHARACTER, RESPONSIBILITY AND SELF-ESTEEM.

Set up a chore chart and allow your child to earn rewards, money, or privileges for the accomplishment of the chores. This technique will not only help kids to feel a great sense of accomplishment when the work is done, but also to become self-disciplined and to develop the confidence that they can make things happen if they work at it.

8. PICTURE A SPECIAL FUTURE FOR YOUR CHILD.

"Wow! With those skills, you'll do great in your game."

"With your love for people, I can imagine you someday being a counselor, a nurse or an occupational therapist." Help your kids to picture themselves accomplishing goals they have set.

A CHALLENGE TO YOU:

1. On a scale of 1 to 10, with 10 being highest, rate your self-esteem. If it's low, how did it get that way? Take steps to enhance your self-esteem through reading, seminars, workshops and counseling.

2. Which method of building one's self-esteem will you concentrate on during the next few weeks? Make a plan and stick to it, then pick another area to concentrate on.

HELPING YOUR PRETEEN DEAL WITH STRESS

It's little wonder that children and teenagers today experience a lot of stress. One only need look at the newspaper each day to identify a few of the reasons. The American Medical Association recently released its first "National Report Card on Violence," and the overall grade for America was a *D*. Wars, bombings, murders, and kidnappings are daily occurrences and are covered extensively in the newspapers and by television networks. Additionally, kids experience the stress of achieving in school and sports, "making it" socially and belonging to a peer group, meeting their parents' and teachers' expectations, dealing with peer pressure to experiment with drugs and alcohol. The increasing rates of teenage suicides and the use of drugs and alcohol by preteens and teenagers are further indicators of our need to help our kids deal more effectively with stress. As parents, we need to be more deliberate in this endeavor.

KNOW THE SYMPTOMS

The first thing parents need to be aware of in helping kids deal with stress is the wide range of symptoms that can be due to stress.

Parents often become upset by the symptoms and do not consider the underlying reasons for a child's behavior.

The following is a partial list of stress symptoms:

◆ Physical symptoms include headaches, stomachaches, rashes, loss of appetite, etc.

◆ Emotional symptoms include nightmares, mood changes, apathy, excessive worrying, and negative feelings.

◆ Behavioral symptoms include fighting, yelling, stealing, poor schoolwork, alcohol or drug use.

IDENTIFY STRESSORS

The second step parents can take is to help their kids identify possible stressors they are experiencing.

My youngest daughter, while in high school, wrote out her list of stressors (an exercise I have had her do frequently). Her list included: not playing enough on her school soccer team, lower grades than usual, "stupid" teachers, friends "who dump their problems on me or do things behind my back," her older brother and sister being away at college, ankles and shins that were always sore, and receiving laser treatments for her birthmark. Since most adults deal with a great deal of stress in the "real" world, we sometimes minimize what our kids are having to cope with.

TAKE ACTION

For many years, I have ingrained into my own kids' memories a simple formula for dealing with stress:

The first way to deal with stress is to **take care of yourself**. Be sure to get enough sleep, exercise, relaxation time, and eat the right foods. (Avoid sugar and caffeine,

(Continued on next page.)

(Continued from previous page.)

just to name a couple of things.)

A second way to deal with stress is to **change your attitude** about the stressor. Encourage your child to develop the faith that God allows things to happen for a reason, that good things can come out of bad situations, and to **trust God**. Help kids understand and remember that life is 10 percent what happens to you and 90 percent how you look at it. Getting a bad grade on a test, breaking up with a girlfriend or boyfriend, failing to make a team can be very traumatic for preteens and teenagers. Be sure to accept your children's feelings of disappointment and be sympathetic to them, but also try to help them to look at the disappointment in a more positive way.

The third way to deal with stress is to **take constructive action**.

Studying for a test, practicing for a speech, talking to a teacher about a problem, getting a tutor to help with a subject, or writing a letter expressing one's feelings to a friend who has let one down are all examples of taking constructive action in dealing with stress.

Sometimes, however, these first three suggestions are just not enough. When our daughter Robyn was struggling with an Advanced Placement Physics class, we tried all three of these suggestions and nothing seemed to help, so she switched to a different class. Sometimes the best thing to do is to simply **eliminate the stressor**. Eliminating an extracurricular activity because a kid is on overload, helping a child to stay away from "friends" who do not build him or her up, and changing teachers at school are all examples of eliminating a stressor. Unfortunately, many stressors cannot be eliminated, but parents need to help their kids figure out when a stressor *should* be eliminated.

Some time ago I noticed on one of Chrissy's lists of stressors and possible ways to deal with each one that she had listed a fifth way to deal with stress. It's probably the most important one of all, and could fall under the category of taking constructive action, but it deserves a category of its own. Chrissy wrote down that the fifth way to deal with stress was to **PRAY**. Teach your kids to pray and to trust that their prayers will be answered, so that the first thing out of their mouths is "Dear God...." Remember to point out when prayers are answered, and reinforce your confidence that God will always give us what we need. He may not give us what we want or what we *think* we want, but He will give us what we need.

Teaching kids concrete and practical ways to deal with stress is one of the most important challenges you will undertake as a parent. The time to begin is *now*, and the effort should continue throughout and beyond the high-school years.

A CHALLENGE TO YOU:

1. Which of the stress symptoms listed above (or other stress symptoms) has your preteen been demonstrating?

2. Sit down with your child and help him or her to identify the things that are causing stress.

3. Discuss the five ways to deal with stress, and help your child determine which of the techniques will be best to use with each stressor (more than one technique may be appropriate). At least every four to five months, help your kids complete this task, even if you have to add a few bucks to their allowances to get them to take the time!

DEVELOPING YOUR CHILD'S RELATIONSHIP WITH GOD

If you're reading this article, I am sure you recognize and accept the importance of your child's developing faith and relationship with God. However, you may have become disenchanted, hurt or discouraged by someone or some church institution that has turned you away from a relationship with God. For those of you who have been hurt or let down by the church and/or someone in the church, it will be important for you to deal with these issues before you will be able to help your child develop a faith in a loving God.

Always remember that faith is meant to *grow*. Do not compare yourself to Billy Graham, but remember that as you study God's Word, hear God's Word, and speak God's words, your faith *will* grow.

When I was a child my father never went to church. My mother took my brother and me, while my father stayed at home. We never prayed at dinner time and we always took the summer off from going to church. I also remember feeling that my church was only after money because they had a board up in the front of the church that always had numbers on it: 378, 258, 425, etc. The numbers changed every week and I assumed that the numbers represented the amount of money that had been raised the week before, and we were being encouraged to donate more this week. I was an adult before I learned what those numbers really were—they were the numbers of the hymns we were singing that week!

Situations and assumptions like those I have just described can become tremendous barriers to parents as they desire to help their kids develop a faith in God.

MODEL YOUR FAITH

One of the most crucial contributions you can make in helping your child to develop faith in God is for you, as his or her parent, to model a positive, healthy relationship with God. At a recent Father's Day service at our church, one man read, "Your greatest responsibility as a father is to show your children what God the Father is really like." What an awesome responsibility this is—for both fathers and mothers! Our children's behavior will model our behavior. If we model trust in God, they will be more likely to develop that trust; if we feel loved and worthwhile because we are children of God, then they will feel loved and worthwhile; if we trust that God has everything under control and works good through all things, then they will likely develop those same attitudes.

KEEP GROWING

In a practical, everyday way, there are definitely things parents can do to enhance their kids' relationships with God.

Try these practical suggestions:

1. Model for your children the importance of studying the Bible. Over the years, my wife and I have both attended weekly Bible studies. During the past two years, we have both been trying to read

(Continued on next page.)

(Continued from previous page.)

through the Bible in a year, and we let our children know how we are doing in meeting this goal.

2. Pray with your children on a regular basis, at dinner time and/or before they go to bed at night. Pray also on special occasions, such as prior to leaving for a trip, or before a big meeting at work, or before they are to take a test in school, or just in everyday situations where you sense God's help is needed.

3. On index cards, write answers to prayer; periodically go through the cards and read them aloud to remind yourselves of God's faithfulness.

4. Encourage your children to memorize Bible verses. Share with them verses that have been helpful to you.

5. Attend church on a regular basis, and do not make church attendance an option to be discussed each week. If your child spends the night somewhere on Saturday night, arrange to pick him or her up before church—if possible, taking the friend along.

6. Make sure that as your pre-teens enter the teen years, they have made connections with a positive youth group that will provide support, instruction and assistance in helping them (and you!) navigate the teen years.

Remember, parents: There is only one perfect parent, and that is our Father in Heaven. We will always fall short of Him, but we can strive to help our kids develop a close relationship with Him by taking corrective action now. Don't let guilt keep you from doing what's right, and it's never too late to do what's right!

A CHALLENGE TO YOU:

1. If you have drifted away from a close relationship with God, try to identify the reasons why, then deal with those issues constructively, possibly through counseling, to reunite with God.

2. Pick one or two of the suggestions listed above and begin to apply it in helping your child develop faith in God.

3. Talk with your preteen about something you are doing in a positive way regarding your faith; don't leave it up to chance that your child will see it for him- or herself.

MY KIDS ONLY THINK ABOUT THEMSELVES!

Throughout the years of my counseling practice I have observed many adults that were not taught as young children how to be sympathetic. Their lack of sympathy not only makes it very difficult for them to be sympathetic to others, but they also tend to have difficulty being sympathetic to themselves, and in allowing others to be sympathetic to them. Lack of sympathy can be devastating to relationships, as well as making it extremely difficult for an individual to get through difficult situations, such as poor health, loss of a job, mid-life transitions, etc.

Many people, including trained professionals, falsely assume that all adults instinctively know how to be sympathetic. They act as if sympathy is something a person catches, like a cold or the flu; either you have it or you don't. They don't understand that sympathy can be—in fact, *must* be taught and learned.

Some children are by nature sympathetic towards a person they perceive as hurting. However, for the most part, parents need to make a conscious and conscientious effort to teach their children and teenagers how to be sympathetic.

SOME PRACTICAL WAYS TO TEACH SYMPATHY ARE:

1. **Model sympathy to your spouse and children** by asking how their days went, doing one of their chores if they are sick, doing something special for them when they are down in the dumps, etc.

2. **Emphasize the need for your kids to complete chores,** not only as a way to earn money for their needs but because it will help you by relieving some of your workload.

3. **Praise acts of sympathy** and apply negative consequences

when your children do not show sympathy. For example, set an earlier bedtime for your kids if they have not been quiet and allowed a sick person to rest.

4. **Let your kids know how you are feeling** and what they can do to help you. Don't keep your feelings in, attempting to act strong if you are feeling weak. If you are sick or discouraged about a project that is not going well, let your kids know.

5. **Help your children to actively consider the needs of others.** Encourage them to send a card to a fellow student that is sick, donate some of their toys to a local charity, or give out birthday party invitations privately and not at school where all who were not invited can observe.

6. **As you watch TV shows together, point out examples** in which people are not sympathetic to one another.

7. **Expect respect and sympathy** from your kids. Don't do things over and over for them without also receiving from them in return. Some parents

(Continued on next page.)

(Continued from previous page.)

(especially mothers) tend to do and do for their kids without getting anything in return. Some kids will only learn to be sympathetic if you are firm with them. Refuse to drive them someplace if they have not completed a chore you asked them to do. Be sure to tell them why you won't drive them, and encourage them to think of your needs next time.

8. **Involve your children in community activities** that foster their concern for the welfare of others. Encourage them to contribute a portion of their allowance to your church; join walks for hunger or other causes; bring food to a needy person and take the kids with you; encourage them to go on short-term mission trips when they enter the teenage years.

A CHALLENGE TO YOU:

1. Were your mother and father sympathetic to each other when you were a child? Were they sympathetic to you?

2. Were you taught how to be sympathetic as a child?

3. Select two or three of the ideas listed above and make a conscious effort to implement those ideas; then try several other ideas.

LIVING WITH THE SECOND-GREATEST INFLUENCE ON YOUR CHILD

Before discussing the second-greatest influence on a child, it's important to acknowledge the greatest influence on a child. Believe it or not, the greatest influence on a child's life is that of his or her parents. When asked what the second-greatest influence is, most parents will respond, "teachers," "peers," "television," "the media," or "heroes." None of these is correct.

The second-greatest influence on a child is **congenital temperament**—or traits that your child was born with. Many women recognize differences in their children before they are even born by the way they react *in utero*. Certain temperaments are not only congenital (present at birth), but are basic characteristics of a child and may stay with him or her throughout life. These traits can be modified by a child's environment, but may change only with difficulty, or not at all.

TEMPERAMENT TRAITS

Ross Campbell describes nine different temperament traits in his book, *How to Really Love Your Child* (Victor Books, 1977).

◆ **Activity level** is the degree of motor activity a child exhibits, and determines how active or passive he or she is.

◆ **Rhythmicity** is the predictability of such functions as hunger, feeding pattern, and sleep-wake cycle.

◆ **Approach or withdrawal** is the nature of a child's response to a new situation.

◆ **Adaptability** is the speed and ease with which a current behavior is able to be modified by a new situation.

◆ **Intensity** of reaction is the amount of energy used in mood expression.

◆ **Threshold of responsiveness** is the intensity level of stimulus required to make a response. (For some kids, a small toy will illicit a loud squeal of joy, while for others it may take a $50 gift to get a faint smile.)

◆ **Quality of mood** refers to whether a child's basic mood is positive, playful, joyful, or negative, unpleasant, unfriendly.

◆ **Distractibility** identifies the effect of extraneous environment on direction of ongoing behavior.

◆ **Attention span and persistence** is the length of time an activity is pursued by a child, and the continuation of an activity in the face of obstacles.

As a parent, you need to recognize these traits and, in many cases, accept the traits. You also need to understand how your own temperament fits or does not fit with your child's. When the fit is good—when parents and kids are similar in temperament—then relationships can be easier. However, when temperament traits are vastly different, conflicts and misunderstandings can result. These differ-

(Continued on next page.)

(Continued from previous page.)

ences (*not* rights and wrongs) can cause a lot of frustration. For example, when my younger daughter got up every morning singing and smiling, it drove me crazy, because I am not a morning person!

CHANGES

You also need to understand the changes that may take place in your child, as early as age 11 or 12, in order to be able to deal with these behaviors more effectively. It is *normal* for preteens and teenagers to: experience rapid physical growth, search for peer acceptance, fluctuate from wanting your help to wanting to do everything themselves, question your ideas that they previously simply accepted, and experience severe mood swings. Some people have even described teenagers as being very similar to two-year-olds who constantly say no; aren't afraid of bodily dirt; are independent, but dependent. The only problem with the analogy is that two-year-olds are cute, while teenagers with their bad attitudes tend not to be cute and lovable.

What do these changes mean on top of the personality traits listed above? For one thing, if preteens act overemotional or irrational, do not attempt to discuss things calmly and rationally, because they will go to great lengths to justify their positions. Wait until they are calmer to discuss things; that may take two minutes or two hours, but be patient.

I hope it's at least comforting to realize that the changes you are observing are normal and to be expected. I used to be considered an expert on teenagers. Then I had three teenagers, and I was no longer an expert. Characteristics of teenagers that I had lectured about for so many years took on new meaning when I was confronted with them on a daily basis. With patience and understanding and the proper parenting tools, we have navigated through the teenage years in a positive fashion and you will be able to do the same.

A CHALLENGE TO YOU:

1. Describe and contrast the temperaments of you and your child using the temperament traits described above.

2. What characteristics of teenagers have you already observed in your preteen?

HOW DO i HELP MY PRETEEN DEAL WiTH PAIN?

When you were hurting as a child, how did you deal with your pain? If your parents divorced, or a parent died when you were young, did you talk about your pain with someone else over a period of time? If kids were mean to you at school, or you lost an election or failed to make a sports team, how did you deal with your pain? Did you talk to your mom and dad about your pain, or did you stuff it and pretend that things were OK?

In my first book, *Dragon Slaying for Parents*, I discussed eight different hidden factors that can interfere with a parent's ability to apply parenting strategies effectively and consistently. These factors may cause parents to become overemotional and attempt to change their children's behavior through anger or intimidation. In my second book, *Dragon Slaying for Couples*, I identified what I consider to be the biggest "dragon" of them all—the tendency to pretend when we are in pain.

CHiLDiSH WAYS

First Corinthians 13:11 says, "When I was a child, I talked like a child, I thought like a child, I reasoned like a child. When I became a man, I put childish ways

behind me." Unfortunately, many of us never did put childish ways behind us.

Childish ways are actions that keep us from getting close to each other, while adult strategies help us to get closer to others. Putting our pain away and pretending it is

not there will not allow us to get close to others. Sharing our pain, our grief, and our anger will help us to get close to those who are able and willing to be sympathetic to our feelings.

Many adults were taught to pretend when in pain as children, rather than to express it. My own father limped around for over six months, unable to reach down and retrieve a golf ball from the cup. When asked what the problem was, he'd usually reply,

"Nothing's wrong, I'm OK." Months later my mother got him into an emergency room for another problem, and upon X-raying his foot, the doctors found a sewing needle he had stepped on in the house!

Many of our parents actually felt that pretending when they were in pain was the right thing to do; they were taught that if you don't talk about painful things, they will go away. Consequently, most adults are walking around with wounds that have not healed. Then when something happens in the present, even though the event may be minor, the old wound is touched and a great deal more pain is expressed than seems warranted.

There's a framed piece of stitchery in my office that says, "You can't heal a wound by saying it's not there." Pretending when in pain prevents us from healing those old wounds. It also prevents us from taking action to correct situations in the present. We may simply say, "Oh, it's not so bad that we fight all the time; it could be worse," or "Summer is almost here—we won't need to worry about school problems in a few weeks."

(Continued on next page.)

(Continued from previous page.)

DEALING WITH PAIN

Your task as a parent is not to prevent your kids from having pain—that is impossible. Your job is to help them to deal with that pain: to help them be angry, to help them cry, to help them grieve the death of a pet or a grandparent. Helping our children to grieve and cry is a tool that will serve them well for a lifetime.

Before you will be able to do this, however, you will first have to look at what you were taught as a child, and put in the time (and it will take time) to learn some new tools or strategies. When your children express pain, accept their feelings, don't just jump in and try to fix it. For instance, if a grandparent dies, don't say, "But look at all the great years we had together." Instead, say, "Boy, I bet you are really sad that you won't see grandpa any more."

Grieving and dealing with pain takes time, it takes tears, it takes hugs, it takes comforting. It takes lots of things, but the ability to deal with pain is a gift you need to give to your children.

A CHALLENGE TO YOU:

1. Think back to your childhood and a time when you felt pain; how were you taught to deal with that pain?

2. Think about some pain that your child has recently gone through. Get him or her to talk about it some more. If he or she doesn't seem able to talk about it, it's OK to say something like, "I'll bet it really made you feel sad when your pet died. You must really miss her." You'll be surprised at how much good that will do.

WHY DO i HAVE TO NAG ABOUT CHORES?

I used to think one of the most important questions to ask parents when their kids were having difficulties at school was whether or not the kids had chores to do at home. That is an important question; however, experience has taught me that a more important question is, "Do they do their chores without nagging and reminding?"

Often, kids who are having difficulties in school and in life are not held accountable to do chores at home, but are instead nagged into doing their chores. Then they go to school expecting to be nagged by teachers to complete their work. Nagging may take place in elementary school, but by the time kids hit middle school and high school, nagging will be less and less prevalent. If a child has not learned to internalize that self-discipline, the logical consequences will be failure. Adults that were nagged as children may have a great deal of difficulty in initiating actions on their own. They may still count on someone or some agency nagging them before they take care of business.

CONSEQUENCES

Quite often when parents nag their children to complete assignments, kids will dawdle and procrastinate. Parents need first of all to state the rule regarding the completion of chores. Describe the chore in specific details and state the consequences, both for completion and non-completion

of chores by an agreed-upon time. For example, state, "If you have completed four of your five chores by 6:00 p.m., then you can watch an hour of TV tonight; if not, then there will be no TV and you'll need to go to bed an hour earlier." Then stand back and follow through.

Typically, kids will test you right away (or within a few days) to see if you'll stick to your guns. They may neglect their chores.

Often parents fear that the technique is not working and go back to the nagging. *Resist that temptation*—it will not result in positive, long-term results. When parents stop nagging about grades, a child's grades may actually drop even further at first. But if you hang in there and apply appropriate positive and negative consequences to school performance, the grades will usually take an upswing.

One rule at our house when our daughter, Robyn, was in high school was that all of her chores had to be done by Friday night; otherwise she had to do the chores on Saturday without getting paid. This consequence was very effective. Unfortunately for Robyn, there were times when she did chores without getting paid. However, my wife and I were able to stay calm and follow through with the consequences. We worked hard to not nag and remind her each day that Friday was only a few days away.

CONTROL AND CODEPENDENCY

Parents who came from an alcoholic or otherwise dysfunctional family will tend to simply

(Continued on next page.)

(Continued from previous page.)

react to their children's misbehavior, rather than taking action. They'll scream and yell rather than setting up a chore chart. They will also attempt to control their children, always trying to get them to do the "right" thing, rather than realizing the importance of allowing children to make their own choices or mistakes and then following through with consequences.

Codependency is a 1990s buzzword to describe the traits of those adults who were brought up in dysfunctional families. Counseling and support groups may be necessary to help overcome the tendencies mentioned.

Some parents also nag because that is what they learned from their parents. They may simply be recreating an environment similar to the one they grew up in which is very normal to them, although very unhealthy.

A CHALLENGE TO YOU:

1. Do you find yourself nagging your children to complete chores? Think back to your childhood to help you determine why you have developed this pattern.

2. Set up a chore chart system. Spell out the chores and then set up rewards if the chores are completed and consequences if they are not completed.

PARENTS: HOW DO YOU PARENT YOURSELF?

Most parents strive very hard to do the right things with their kids. They will read books on parenting, and attend seminars on how to deal with teenagers. However, many parents will often avoid thinking about or considering what kind of a parent they are being to *themselves*. A challenge for all parents is to "go the distance"—hang in there through all the trials and tribulations of parenting; enjoy the good times and deal appropriately with the stressful times. But in order to go the distance, you need to take care of yourself.

ARE YOU TAKING GOOD CARE OF YOURSELF?

According to one model of counseling, each of us can be divided into three parts: a parent, an adult, and a child.

The adult in each of us is the fact-oriented or unemotional part of our personality. The *child* in each of us is the emotional part of our personality; it has needs and requires nurturing. The *parent* in each of us consists of our beliefs, our values, and our "shoulds." Some people also refer to the *parent* as the part that contains our "tapes," or messages that we picked up as children and therefore we may assume these messages to be valid without ever questioning them.

A simple example might help tie these three together. Years ago when I was having chest pains, I realized I needed to relax more. The *adult* in me definitely knew I needed to relax. However, when I would begin to relax, the *parent* in me would say, "Hey! You need to be doing something; you aren't being productive!" and immediately I would begin to do something. I needed to examine the message I picked up as a child that says one needs to work to be an OK person. I had to recognize that message and consistently attack it in order to make it change, and only then could my behavior change.

Often, we aren't even aware that we are operating under the influence of those old messages, and we do not attack the message long enough for it to change. However, we will not be able to change behaviors unless we change some beliefs, or messages we picked up.

NURTURE OR CRITICISM?

We are all parenting ourselves every day. The problem is that most adults are very *critical parents* to themselves, rather than being *nurturing parents* to themselves. Most parents will parent themselves in the same way they were parented as children. If you were criticized as a youth, or if your needs were not given importance, then you will tend to parent yourself in the same fashion unless you break the cycle. The positive things you are striving to do for your children are the very things you need to do for yourself!

Do you praise yourself when you have done something well, or do you tend to only criticize yourself for mistakes made?

(Continued on next page.)

(Continued from previous page.)

Do you set realistic goals for yourself to accomplish in a given time period, or are you overwhelmed by your list of "shoulds" that never get done to your satisfaction?

Are you sympathetic to yourself when you are sick or tired, and take care of yourself, or do you tend to drive yourself to achieve more and more?

Have you forgiven yourself for past mistakes, or do you continue to condemn yourself for mistakes that you made in the past?

Do you occasionally buy things that you need, or get yourself gifts, or do you tend to spend all your money on clothes and things for your kids?

BALANCE

Is your life in balance (spiritual, physical, social, personal, children, marriage, friends, professional, volunteer work) or do you tend to devote all your time and attention to just one or two areas?

Some time ago, a person I counseled with asked me how much longer he would have to

"do this." When I said, "The rest of your life," he became upset and almost dropped out of counseling prematurely, because he did not want to be in counseling the rest of his life! What I meant, however, was that he would need to strive to be a nurturing, positive parent to himself for the rest of his life.

You will make progress in your efforts, but you will also slip back at times. Don't be discouraged by the slips; instead, accept them as normal and natural, and as a reminder of what you must do.

A CHALLENGE TO YOU:

1. Think back to your family of origin. How did your parents parent you? Were they nurturing or critical? Are you parenting yourself in the same fashion now?

2. Pick one of the areas described above and work consciously on that area before moving on to another area.

DEVELOPING A DE-PARENTING PLAN

Parenting is a little like flying a kite. If you hold on to the kite too long without letting out string, the string will break. However, if you let out string too quickly, the kite will fall. If we do not let go of our children at an appropriate time, their rebellion will be very difficult to deal with. Conversely, if we let go too quickly, they may get into situations that are unhealthy, and may suffer physical and/or emotional harm. In either extreme, children's self-esteem will suffer.

As parents, we need to give up power willingly before kids decide to take it. A very helpful exercise to do periodically with your preteen is to write down and renegotiate current rules. The rules may cover a variety things, such as: bedtime, curfew time, allowance, chores, care of room, use of makeup, dating, and church attendance. Discuss the rules and any changes either of you feels might be appropriate. See if you can negotiate changes in rules so that both you and your child win. Then decide on a time when you will review the rules together again (birthdays are one good choice).

LET GO GRADUALLY

As children get older, more and more areas need to be turned over to them and left to their judgment. If a child proves he or she cannot make wise decisions in a particular area, then that area may temporarily have to revert to the parent's control.

Especially in the preteen and teenage years, it's important for parents to pick battles carefully— pick "the hills you will die on," so to speak. At some point, turn over responsibility for the care of your child's room, allowing him or her to make the choices in that area. At another point, let your child set his or her bedtime. At some point, let kids decide what they will do with their hair. There are more important areas to be con-

cerned with than these minor areas that have potential for prolonged and painful conflict, especially in the teen years.

CONSTRUCTIVE SOLUTIONS

Look for constructive solutions to areas that easily turn into power struggles. One creative solution to clothes woes might be to give your preteen a clothing allowance. Each month, budget an amount of money that your child may use for clothes. Let him or her begin to make decisions about how to spend this money. You may be amazed at how many ways this simple strategy will help: You will become less concerned about a messy room and whether or not your child is ruining clothes by leaving them all over his or her room; if your child loses clothes or ruins them, it's his or her responsibility.

Another good way to encourage responsibility might be to set up paid chores that can be done any time during the week. Chores such as vacuuming, ironing, mowing the lawn, dusting, and washing the car would fit in this category. Choose a certain day of the week by which the chores must be fin-

(Continued on next page.)

(Continued from previous page.)

ished; if the chore is not done by that day, then the child does it the next day without getting paid. Don't nag, don't remind and don't react with yelling or guilt-producing statements—just follow through with the consequences.

If kids constantly wait to be reminded to do things, they will inevitably experience difficulties in middle school, high school and the rest of their lives, since there will be fewer and fewer people to remind them to complete their responsibilities.

Letting go by turning over responsibility to your child will not only help to enhance your child's self-esteem, but will also serve to minimize the conflicts and rebellion so often associated with the preteen and teenage years. Remember that successful parenting through these years is not simply a matter of luck, but of acquiring the skills to handle the challenges effectively.

One of my favorite reflections on letting go is the following poem.

LEARNING THE BICYCLE

The older children pedal past
Stable as little gyros, spinning hard
To supper, bath, and bed, until at last
We also quit, silent and tired
Beside the darkening yard where trees
Now shadow up instead of down.
Their predictable lengths can only tease
Her as, head lowered, she walks her bike alone
Somewhere between her wanting to ride
And her certainty she will always fall.

Tomorrow, though I will run behind,
Arms out to catch her, she'll tilt then balance wide
Of my reach, 'till distance makes her small,
Smaller, beyond the place I stop and know
That to teach her I had to follow
And when she learned I had to let her go.

(Wyatt Prunty, "Learning the Bicycle" (for Heather), The American Scholar, 58 no. 1 (Winter 1989): 122. Used by permission of the author.)

A CHALLENGE TO YOU:

1. Think back to your childhood. Did your parents let go or did they hold on too long? Did they negotiate rules with you? If not, these areas will be challenges to consider as you attempt to change your behavior with your children.

2. List all the areas for which you have established rules with your child. Next, write down your idea of an appropriate rule, and have your child do the same. Then discuss the rules and attempt to negotiate a win/win situation. In some situations you may have to simply say no to a request, but don't be too quick to jump to that response without considering whether or not an item is negotiable.

CLiP ART

Clip art can be a wonderful way
to enhance and decorate fliers,
church bulletins, folders, forms and posters.
Cut and paste the following illustrations
to add interest to newsletters,
or all kinds of announcements.

ADDITIONAL RESOURCES FOR TEACHERS

INTRODUCING PLANET 56

Gospel Light's All New Sunday School Curriculum for 5th and 6th Graders

Finally today's new generation of 5th and 6th graders have a curriculum of their own. **Planet 56** takes kids through 24 Scripture passages they can't live without—giving them God's perspective on making friends, getting along in their families, dealing with failure, improving communication and more!

Planet 56 features exciting options that take Sunday School lessons home— the **Bible in Your Brain** Scripture memory music, **Planet 56 Comics** take-home papers and **Bible Sleuth CD-ROM** game.

Check it out today. **Planet 56** is so much fun that kids will wonder why it's called Sunday "School"!

AUDIOTAPES

15 Minute Teacher Training

Today's life in the fast lane makes it almost impossible to schedule teacher training. These concentrated training tapes sum up the essentials of effective teaching in 15-minute bites, making them perfect for teachers on the move. Topics included are discipline, how to talk to children about salvation, understanding children and how to converse with children. Each set comes with two 30-minute audiotapes and is reproducible for you to provide a set to each of your teachers. SPCN 25116.03411

CLIP ART BOOKS & DISKS

The Big Picture Bible Time Line Book

These reproducible pages make a 60-foot time line showing the sequence of events in the Bible. Use for coloring activities or place around the room to help children track their progress through Scripture. ISBN 08307.14723

Bible Story Clip Art on Disk

Makes your lessons, flyers and handouts come alive. Includes pictures of Bible events, characters and places.

SPCN 25116.08952 Win.
SPCN 25116.08944 Mac.

The Kids' Workers' Clip Art Book

Over 1,000 reproducible illustrations for teachers and others who love to work with kids. ISBN 08307.15207

The One Minute Poster Book

A dream come true for anyone who needs to publicize an event at church. It contains pre-made posters and flyers for every church event imaginable. ISBN 08307.14421

The Sunday School Clip Art Book

Produce great looking mailers, flyers, letters, invitations, brochures and announcements for your Sunday School. Follow the step-by-step instructions. ISBN 08307.11147

BOOKS

Everything You Want to Know About Teaching Children, Grades 1—6

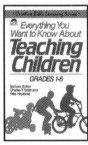

by Barbara Bolton, Charles T. Smith and Wes Haystead

This handbook is designed to give the new as well as the experienced teacher fresh insights and practical plans for effectively teaching God's Word. ISBN 08307.12712

These resources are available from your Christian supplier.

INDEX FOR GAMES